The Bliss Mistress Guide to Transforming the Ordinary into the Extraordinary

Edie Weinstein

Edited by Pamela Maliniak

Artwork and Photography by Cynthia Greb © 2011

BALBOA PRESS
A DIVISION OF HAY HOUSE

Copyright © 2011 by Edie Weinstein

All rights reserved. No part of this book may be used or reproduced by any means, graphic, electronic, or mechanical, including photocopying, recording, taping or by any information storage retrieval system without the written permission of the publisher except in the case of brief quotations embodied in critical articles and reviews.

Balboa Press books may be ordered through booksellers or by contacting:

Balboa Press
A Division of Hay House
1663 Liberty Drive
Bloomington, IN 47403
www.balboapress.com
1-(877) 407-4847

Because of the dynamic nature of the Internet, any web addresses or links contained in this book may have changed since publication and may no longer be valid. The views expressed in this work are solely those of the author and do not necessarily reflect the views of the publisher, and the publisher hereby disclaims any responsibility for them.

The author of this book does not dispense medical advice or prescribe the use of any technique as a form of treatment for physical, emotional, or medical problems without the advice of a physician, either directly or indirectly. The intent of the author is only to offer information of a general nature to help you in your quest for emotional and spiritual well-being. In the event you use any of the information in this book for yourself, which is your constitutional right, the author and the publisher assume no responsibility for your actions.

Any people depicted in stock imagery provided by Thinkstock are models, and such images are being used for illustrative purposes only.
Certain stock imagery © Thinkstock.

ISBN: 978-1-4525-3770-2 (e)
ISBN: 978-1-4525-3768-9 (sc)
ISBN: 978-1-4525-3769-6 (hc)

Library of Congress Control Number: 2011914397

Printed in the United States of America

Balboa Press rev. date: 9/14/2011

Contents

Introduction	The Birth of a Bliss Mistress	1
Chapter 1.	Let's Start at the Very Beginning	7
Chapter 2.	Endless Loop Tape	10
Chapter 3.	As My Own Woman	13
Chapter 4.	Pissing on the Fire	15
Chapter 5.	Fifth Chakra Folly	20
Chapter 6.	A Love Letter to Yourself	25
Chapter 7.	The Servant of the Creation	27
Chapter 8.	Everything I Need To Know, I Learned at Cuddle Party	29
Chapter 9.	And the Year Has Just Begun	34
Chapter 10.	Lila	37
Chapter 11.	Once Wild	40
Chapter 12.	Plugged into Our Source	44
Chapter 13.	A Relationship with Chocolate	47
Chapter 14.	Thoughts That Do No Violence to My Soul	50
Chapter 15.	Standing at the Crossroads	53
Chapter 16.	Tattooed Angel	55
Chapter 17.	The Cosmic Yes!	58
Chapter 18.	Beloved Bozos	61

Chapter 19.	Validation	66
Chapter 20.	Living Orgasmically	68
Chapter 21.	Poetic License	72
Chapter 22.	Dance Like Everyone Is Watching	75
Chapter 23.	Mammogram Mambo	78
Chapter 24.	Mala	81
Chapter 25.	Godwinks	85
Chapter 26.	Zen Starbucks	88
Chapter 27.	Fantabulous 50!	91
Chapter 28.	Blowing Bubbles with Mom	96
Chapter 29.	S'Mores in Heaven	100
Chapter 30.	Bliss Bites	105
AdoRe-sources		108
Chapter 31.	An Interview with His Holiness the Dalai Lama	124
Afterword		130
Bliss Mistress Groups		131
Transform the Ordinary Into the Extraordinary		132
Bliss Bravos		134

Foreword

Yvonne Kaye. Ph.D.

The extraordinary Edie Weinstein asked me to write a foreword for her book about the Bliss Mistress. An honour indeed. I spoke with her, asking what she would like me to highlight. She had some ideas regarding me being one of her mentors (another honour), as well as the essence of the book and a bit about her. She then suggested that if I were unsure, I could read forewords in some other books—just to give me an idea. So I did. I then decided—Nah! Can't do it like that.

This woman is just too unique for me to even consider any other 'foreworder's' comments about other people's work. This is not unusual for me—I do tend to enjoy some level of eccentricity and outrageousness, which is why I recognize a familiar spirit in Edie.

I have been blessed to have known her for many years; I have watched her struggle and overcome so very much in her life. Her courage in turning around tragic experiences into vibrant lessons is astonishing. This is why I decided to write just as I have seen her, still see her, and will continue to see her.

This book, some might feel, is the result of years' growth and change in Edie. It is the culmination of her immense source of creative juices, her learned fearlessness teaching about truth, and her ability to love not only those easy to love, but the unlovable. Quite a feat. This is the book she was meant to write—but only the first. There is no doubt that Edie loves to write, so aren't we lucky to be in at the first publication? It's not just a book about bliss and joyfulness. This is a treatise on overcoming obstacles, some of which would make people shudder. She has written of those situations, and it is important to take heed of them. They were insurmountable it seemed, but then again—we are talking about Edie.

The passion is palpable in her writings. She believes completely in the power of the human spirit, and most brilliantly, she listens. In the day, I was named a 'kick-ass' therapist. Edie was on the receiving end, but goodness, is she a fast learner—and I still have my foot! In this remarkable book, Edie has determined that she will encourage people to understand how to love who they are, and to nurture themselves, because it is vital to do so. Loving, cuddling, talking, stroking—whatever is the preference—Edie can prove to people who are so skeptical that they hurt themselves, that loving and enjoying bliss together with fun and laughter is the great healer of all-time. I teach a course for bereaved people called *Laughing When Nothing Seems Funny*. The beauty of memory, remembering some hilarious incidents that balanced the pain, is a gift from the Universe. Edie is living proof that this is life-changing.

Readers might have to read this delicious book more than once to get the true essence as, although Edie shares details of how to do it, the absence of self worth can be a deterrent of the first order. So if you don't get it once, read it twice or more. As one of my heroes Dr. Viktor Frankl wrote in the Auschwitz concentration camp, "People make conscious decisions on the way they feel." He also wrote, "They can do anything to my body, but they cannot touch my thoughts." Edie has that same philosophy. The beauty of this lovely book is that all can be overcome. *It isn't what life gives you, it's what you do with what life gives you.* While not original to me, I love that phrase; although there might not be cures, there is certainly healing. And it is essential to know that each person has their own story and their own methods. Fabulous. This can be the beginning of new attitudes that make life magnificent and gorgeous—and once begun, it can affect others in our sphere, just like love and laughter do.

Amor Vincit Omnia, Edie-girl. *Love Conquers All.* And so it is. I am so glad you are in my life and in the lives of many others. After this book reaches even more people, your magic will grow. Blessings, and may the joy you bring to others echo in your own sweet and generous soul.

Blissings and Blessings

"I would maintain that thanks are the highest form of thought and that gratitude is happiness doubled by wonder."
—G.K. Chesterton

One of the first things I anticipated doing while writing *Bliss Mistress* was creating this page that shines a brilliant spotlight on those loving souls who so tickle my life. The list could be a book in and of itself so, in advance, I ask forgiveness if your name is not specifically mentioned here. Know that you are in my heart.

First and foremost, I honor my parents, Selma and Moish Weinstein, who obviously were present when the persona of Bliss Mistress was born—this 'alien baby left on their doorstep' who challenged their perception of life and asked all manner of potentially embarrassing questions that they did their best to answer, most of them at the dinner table and many about sex. The joke was that my younger sister didn't need to ask, since I did it first. They provided a warm and loving home and a solid role model for a lifelong loving partnership that lasted nearly 52 years in body and now in Spirit. My Dad died in 2008, and my beautiful Mom joined him the day after Thanksgiving in 2010. They believed in me even when (and especially when), I didn't believe in myself. I am eternally grateful.

My sister, Jan Weinstein Sparta, has been there for me—sometimes gazing at life from an entirely different vantage point. From her, I am learning that my way isn't always the right way, despite what my ego might say! She is, at times, the repository for childhood memories that have slipped my middle-aged mind.

My son, Adam Moser, has been one of my greatest guides. When he was 14, he told me quite emphatically, "Mom, I'm an undercover angel, sent to teach you patience." Now an adult, he's still teaching, and I'm still learning.

My husband, Michael Moser (on the other side since 1998), who loved me deeply and challenged me mightily to grow beyond my self-imposed limitations. Together we created *Visions Magazine,* which we published from 1988—1998, that opened the door to the amazing transformational teachers whose work set the stage for my awakening. Michael's family continues to be part of my life long after his passing.

My longtime (I hesitate to call her my 'old friend') friend, Barbara Cohen, who entered my life on the bench of a pool prior to a swim meet in our teens. She became my 'blood sister' and now refers to me as her 'flower child' friend. She wants to clear my closet of my hippie clothes and take me shopping, à la the television show *What Not To Wear.* Stacy London, are you reading this?

My 'older and wiser cousin', Jody Weiner-Rosenblum, who personifies all the nurturing 'Bubbe love' (but not smother love) of our ancestors, tinged with the playfulness of the child that remains. For all of the late night talks and nightgown dances when we were housemates in our 20's.

Phil Garber and Janet Berkowitz, who continue to astound me with their resilience. Grateful to Phil, in particular, that you and Adam chose each other as 'unofficial Big and Little Brothers'.

My Goddess Retreat Sistahs who have showered me with juicy love and held space for me to laugh, cry, rage, and to speak my truth, even when it wasn't pretty—and who embraced all of me: Ondreah Johnson, Amy Storm, Liz Wright, Dianne Evans, Vicki Dungan, Liora Hill, Gail Hollies, Faith Kremer, Orrie Schulman, Mary LaBarbera, Verna Tweddale, Susan Hageman, Rebecca Berkson, and Jacquie Fajans.

The friends in 'the Sandbox' who offer unconditional love, fun, and frolic.

My 'heart friend' Jaz who coined the name Bliss Mistress and, at just the right time in my life, helped me to slow down and drink of both the beauty within as well as that which surrounds me all the time, inviting me to dance like everyone was watching.

Author and motivational speaker Jim Donovan, who gave me a loving kick in the tush to finish this book, since—as he sagely offered—"The book isn't doing anybody any good in your head."

My cousin and the 'cool older sister' surrogate, Marilyn Alkus Bonomi, who lived with our family while she attended college, for encouraging my writing and always treating me like an adult. Even now, we are in touch through the marvels of modern technology and the phenom of Facebook®.

My all-time favorite teacher, Richard Serfling, who in 6th grade set the bar for excellence and dared me to jump over. It was you too who helped nurture my creativity and passion for writing.

Therapist and author Nancy Dreyfus, who has taught me to 'talk to everyone like they are someone I love', and who fed me just the right words to continue to nourish this book when I felt like I was starving it.

Reid Mihalko and Marcia Baczynski, who created the workshop that allows me to "go to work dressed in pj's, get paid to touch and be touched . . . and it's legal." Cuddle Party™ is now a worldwide phenom.

My spiritual family at Circle of Miracles, Common Ground Fellowship, Center For Conscious Living, and Pebble Hill Church for their constant flow of love that opens doors to commune with the Divine.

Gary Schoenberg, my soul friend and one of my favorite dance partners, whose wisdom comes through in many forms—both playful and profound.

Peggy Tileston who, with her laughter-tinged yogic perspective and deep wisdom, kept me 'sane and vertical' at a job that had me 'immersed in emotion soup' while serving people with mental health diagnoses. To you I say, "Very good, very good . . . YAY!"

Ruth Anne Wood (a.k.a Ruth The Poet) for inspiring me to "take my dreams out of the drawer" and live my peace in addition to introducing me to her concept of 'Scripting for Success'.

Peter Moses, who for years was my creative collaborator in facilitating workshops that offered people the cake and icing too. He calls me "Edie Sweetie" while reminding me to live in the present moment.

Yvonne Kaye, one of my dearest mentors, who taught me that "discipline is freedom," booted my butt into recovery from co-dependence, and knows that humor is nourishment for the heart and soul.

Murray Needleman, whose invitation to accept myself 'as is' and whose perfectly timed calls over the years asking, "How are you, dear heart?" allowed for the leaps it took to write this book.

Sandy Levenson, the "chiropractor with hands and heart of gold," for keeping my spine and soul aligned.

Greg Petitti, who entered my life at a time when I was getting to know myself all over again, who coined the phrase 'Edie moments' to indicate anything miraculous or serendipitous, and who often starts conversations when he wants to pick my brain for resources with the words: "You who know everyone . . ." To that I have replied, "not yet."

The crew from Together, Inc., whose youthful idealism and service in our college years continues now that we are in our 50's. When we have our reunions, it as is if no time has passed. Most especially the resilient Albert Borris, who introduced me to the word *Namaste* way back when—and who truly lives that energy.

Cindy Greb, whose healing hands massage *away* the stress and massage *in* the bliss. A creative soul whose artistry and photography dazzle me. Her beautiful works of he(art) embellish this book, and she and I collaborated on the back cover photo of the author at play.

Arielle Ford and Brian Hilliard, whose loving relationship is a model for what I choose to create in my own. I have told them, "I want what you're having."

Joan Borysenko for her resilience in the face of life challenges as she keeps on keepin' on with her writing, looking to her readers for inspiration to feed her work.

Dr. Judith Orloff, whose amazing ability to merge the worlds of the mainstream and metaphysical through her writing and speaking encourage me to do the same.

To the hundreds of 'movers and shakers' I had the joy and privilege of interviewing over the past 20 plus years including the following: His Holiness the Dalai Lama, Louise Hay, Ram Dass, Shirley MacLaine, Joan Borysenko, Debbie Ford, David Darling, Arielle Ford, Brian Hilliard, Lori Cotler, Glen Velez, Marianne Williamson, Ben & Jerry, Michael Beckwith, Judith Orloff, Darren Weissman, Barry and Joyce Vissell, Neale Donald Walsch, James Twyman, Wayne Dyer, Elizabeth Lesser, Michael Franti, Jean Houston, and Elisabeth Kubler-Ross. Also to the publishers of the magazines and newspapers who have counted me as part of their teams over the years.

Alan Cohen, who has been a friend for more than 30 years and graced the first cover of *Visions Magazine*. Gratitude for reminding me to 'rise in love'. No matter how much time has gone by between our meetings, we just pick up where we left off.

SARK (Susan Ariel Rainbow Kennedy) who, from the moment I read her work, beckoned me to 'live juicy'. Her inspiration colors my life with vibrance and flavors it with sweet succulence.

Karen Drucker, who shares with me a water baby history, a willingness to step into the spotlight—despite trembling knees at times—and a very active and persistent 'inner critic' who responds to Karen's melodic message, "I will be gentle with myself."

Phil Scarito, extraordinary fitness guide who 'saw fit' to introduce me to his sweetie Pam who would become my fabulous editor.

Victor Fuhrman, who honors the Goddess and whose Reiki infused hands and heart bless all those with whom he comes in contact.

Kathy Davis for whose KDD studios I worked/played as one of her 'elves', creating magical greeting cards.

Susan Duval, who shares with me a passion for promotion and the notoriety of knowing anyone I don't know and vice versa.

Barry and Joyce Vissell, who were among the first columnists for *Visions Magazine* and have been shining examples of love lived wondrously.

Molly Nece (a.k.a. Molly Sunshine) for creating The Molly Sunshine Tour where I celebrated my 52nd birthday and for encouraging me to shine my light brightly.

Ken Kaplan, spiritual brother and one of Adam's mentors whose dream interpretive skills have guided me to clarity.

Pamela Maliniak, my marvelous editor, who adopted *Bliss Mistress* after hearing me speak at an event. I knew immediately that she was the one to be the midwife for this book.

To the lovers and friends who have paved the way from where I was to where I am. Love is never wasted, and I honor what we shared and wish you your hearts desires even if we are no longer in each others' daily lives.

The One I have not (at this writing) met but who shares the dance of life with me in a "totally fulfilling, mutually supportive loving partnership."

To you, the reader . . . without you, this lovely book and extension of my very being would be lonely on the shelf. Thanks for adopting *Bliss Mistress* and taking her into your heart and home.

And to "God/Goddess/All That Is" for giving me life and continuing to be the spark of inspiration that ignited my fire.

Infinite Love and Gratitude to you all . . .

Introduction

The Birth of a Bliss Mistress

The seeds for this book were planted long before I put fingers to keyboard. They were present, I imagine, before I even entered this incarnation. I come from a long line of hardy and heart-y explorers and journeyers. My lineage includes Eastern European immigrants who traveled to a 'new world' to escape persecution and embrace opportunity. They were called upon to find ways and means to survive and raise families, relying upon ingenuity and a do-what-it-takes attitude. I honor what it took for my mother's grandparents to raise thirteen children, who in turn raised an entire generation. I acknowledge the courage involved when my Russian immigrant paternal grandparents escaped the persecution of the pogroms to cross the ocean to a land that was fabled to have streets paved with gold. In their case, the riches came more in the form of treasured family connections and sustainable ties than it ever did in green currency.

One inheritance I received from both sides of the family, which I value immensely, is a love of learning. According to my mother, I would always be seen carrying a book—at the dinner table, throughout the day, in the car. She would read to us daily and escort us to the library down the street for story hour. As a child, I spent countless hours in doctors' offices for treating symptoms of asthma. My mother viewed these as creative opportunities to inject knowledge in addition to the allergy serum. She would spell a word, and I would identify it; I would spell a word, and she would tell me its meaning. It eased the tedium of the waiting time and expanded my vocabulary exponentially.

As I have come to accept, it was virtually an impossibility that I escape the delicious fate of becoming a writer. Grammatically incorrect as it is, *I can't NOT write*. It is one of the first things I want to do in the morning and becomes my soporific when I can't sleep. I have been told by many people who have read my tappings and typings over the years that they feel as if they are in the scene with me as I describe my experiences—I take that to be the highest compliment.

Quite simply, writing nourishes my soul. It has also saved my sanity several times while teetering on the edge over the past 52 years. During some of the darkest nights of the soul, what helped me know for certain that the sun would come out tomorrow (as my 'inner Annie' bursts forth in song), were the words that came through me. I often say that my writing 'writes me'; the Muse whispers in my ear daily. And when I disregard her call, she's been known to shout. In the midst of some of the most profound experiences, rather than simply relishing them, I find myself thinking, "How can I tell people about this?" And before you ask—no, it doesn't happen during sex.

The persona of Bliss Mistress was born a few years ago when, on the way into a classroom to teach a workshop called *BYOB—Be Your Own Bliss!*, one of the participants commented, "Oh, you're the Bliss Master."

Telling my friend Jaz about it later, his twinkling-eyed response was, "Oh no—Bliss **Mistress**." It set me to wondering just how one dedicated to the art of bliss would live, and this book was born.

It is my intention to offer you, the reader, a veritable buffet of luscious options, redolent with flavor, brimming with aromas that beckon with waving fingers. Decadent delights to tantalize all your senses. I hold out before you portable life skills that you can put to use immediately in your personal and professional lives. Absorb what feels right for you and leave the rest. In yoga, we talk about the concept of 'going to your edge' so you don't injure yourself. I invite you to go to your edge and then just a wee bit more. Living on the edge can be exhilarating or frightening.

The choice—as always—is yours.

An experience in July of 2008 spoke with undeniable clarity as to which of these two emotional inspirations I needed to elect. For 20 years, I held the journalistic dream of interviewing His Holiness the Dalai Lama. I had been in his presence a few years earlier amongst over 20,000 others at Rutgers Stadium in New Brunswick, NJ. On that day, he wasn't granting media interviews, so the closest I came was writing about the event and interviewing devotees of this man who stands as a tribute to compassionate living.

Fast forward to early summer 2008, and it looked as though my dream had a greater possibility of turning into reality; a friend, Greg Schultz, was charged as the event manager for a visit His Holiness was to make to the Philadelphia area. For a few weeks, Greg had been extending a sense of hope that my request might truly happen.

A week prior to His Holiness' presentation at the Kimmel Center in Philadelphia, my friend Linda Hunter and I attended one of my favorite events—the XPoNential Music Festival. Sponsored by the Philadelphia-based radio station WXPN (88.5 FM), it is held annually on the Camden, NJ waterfront. We were talking with a photographer friend when my cell phone rang; I answered it, little realizing at the time that the voice on the other end intended to deliver a life changing message. It was Greg, and he was asking me to free the dates of July 16th and 17th in order to harvest the bounty of my deeply held vision—along with one other Philadelphia area journalist, I had been granted an audience with the Dalai Lama.

As the words sunk into my sun-soaked brain, I screamed into the phone. The moment was captured magnificently by our photographer friend and now sits on my dresser as a reminder that anything is possible. When I describe the feelings behind the experience, I say that I was "somewhere between holy shit abject terror and orgasmic bliss." When in doubt, go for the orgasmic bliss.

And then 'impostor syndrome' kicked in. According to wikipedia:

> *Regardless of what level of success they may have achieved in their chosen field of work or study or what external proof they may have of their competence, those with the syndrome remain convinced internally they do not deserve the success they have achieved and are actually frauds. Proof of success is dismissed as luck, timing, or as a result of deceiving others into thinking they were more intelligent and competent than they believe themselves to be.*

The chattering monkey mind began its free-for-all . . . *What if you really aren't that competent a writer? What if after all these years of wanting this, you don't have anything of value to say? What if you let down all of the people who believe in you?* And then I firmly, but lovingly, quieted the clamorous chimp with a symbolic banana. I reminded her that I wouldn't have been offered this opportunity if I wasn't a competent writer who had earned her chops.

Know that even after the magnificence of the time with His Holiness and the articles that were born of that experience, as I write this book a few years later, the feelings have arisen afresh. The sneering simian glares at me, eyes narrowing, teeth bared: *Who are you to write this book?* On occasion, I develop spiritual amnesia, and I am guessing that you do as well. In the midst of this spiritual amnesia—forgetting who I really am—someone or some experience inevitably shows up to remind me of my sole/soul identity. Here, I recall the Marianne Williamson quote in *A Return to Love: Reflections on the Principles of 'A Course in Miracles'*: "You are a child of the universe. Your playing small doesn't serve the world . . . As we let our own light shine, we unconsciously give other people permission to do the same."

With the call to write comes the agreement to be vulnerable. It's a trade-off I willingly make. I open the door and invite you to enter into my world—the sweet and the sour, the marvelous and the messy, the blessings and the bitchiness. It's part and parcel of who we all are, like it or not.

This book is a distillation of my experiences for the past half century and perhaps eons before. There are times when I wish I had the ability to orchestrate a Vulcan mind meld and simply download all of the information directly to your consciousness; but for now, this way will have to suffice. It seems more appropriate that a book on bliss be savored and enjoyed at your leisure anyway.

Like many of you who will be turning these pages, I proudly claim the designation of 'Cultural Creative'. According to the website www.culturalcreatives.org, we are: "literally creating a new culture"; we purchase "ecologically sustainable products and services"; and we have "concern for the whole planet." We "insist on authenticity" in all aspects of our lives. We are "bringing women's issues [and spirituality] into public life."

Also like many of you, I am a Renaissance woman and work in progress: journalist, speaker, interfaith minister, social worker, massage/energy worker, networking queen and clown . . . yes, no clownin' around, you read correctly. She is one of my alter egos—a character named Feather who is a faerie. Her wings are vivid purple and red, with streamers and feathers pluming downward. Born at a time when I needed laughter as a healing balm for my emotional wounds, she is ever evolving: sometimes edgy and a bit naughty, sometimes childlike and silly.

The book is divided into 30 chapters, one for each day of the month. Each one has a story to tell, with grow-it-yourself exercises to do at your pace. Sometimes we need to take tiny nibbles of pleasure before we are ready to drink it down in gulps, and there are moments when we prefer the sweetness of a kiss planted on our waiting lips. At the end of each chapter, I've included **Bliss Kisses**—these questions might serve as tempting little pecks on the cheek that leave you giggling with delight, or they might serve as soul searching smooches that make you swoon in ecstasy with what you discover. At the end of the book, I've included quotable tidbits called **Bliss Bites**—these delicious little nibbles are fat, calorie, and cholesterol free treats in which you can indulge at your leisure. Take your pick!

Open to a chapter at random and hear what speaks to you. Sit with the imagery and the questions. Some of the stories were written a few years ago, and some are more recent. I view them as stepping stones on which I leap from place to place, as well as the Hansel and Gretel breadcrumb trail that wound inexorably to this moment.

At the back of the book is a list of resources for your ongoing education and en-lightening-up. These are people and organizations who have inspired my bliss and enriched my life immeasurably.

The butterfly that embellishes the cover is a reminder that we are all in an ever evolving state of transformation, coming out of our chrysalis and spreading our wings to soar over the horizon. It is also in cherished memory of my mother, Selma Weinstein, who suggested that image and told me, before she crossed over on November 26, 2010, that she would come back as a butterfly.

The feather that invites you into the book is there for several reasons. The first is related to the faerie-clown that I referenced earlier. The next touches one of my favorite movies, *Forrest Gump*, with the feather that drifts about during some of the scenes. As a character unto itself, it suggests that life may happen at random and may also bring us to the right place at the right time, as it seemed to do for Forrest. That brings me to a book dear to my heart—*Illusions* by Richard Bach. This pivotal read in my early spiritual evolution/revolution introduces a feather as representation of manifestation. Lastly, I give out feathers at many of the workshops I teach to remind you to lighten up and tickle your fancy—or whatever else you have in mind.

I see the book as a conversation between the two of us, reading it as you sit or lie down someplace supremely comfortable, perhaps a sweet-tooth pleasing treat by your side.

Wishing you Blissings and Blessings,

Edie

Chapter 1

Let's Start at the Very Beginning

To get to your destination, you first need to be aware of exactly where your feet are planted. Are they in lush green grass that tickles your toes? Hot, sticky tar? Suck-you-down-into-the-muck quicksand?

In order to make sure we are all on the same page (and as you are reading this, apparently we are), let's define a few key words:

> **BLISS:** Walking on clouds, floating on air, all without benefit of invisible fishing wire or tightrope; a goosebumps experience that has you giggling with delight; a sense of *ahhh* and awe simultaneously

> **TRANSFORMING:** Abracadabra; presto-change-o; alchemical process that turns lead into gold

> **ORDINARY:** Black and white and shades of gray; customary; day-to-day

> **EXTRAORDINARY:** *Ta-da!*; Highly exceptional and remarkable; amazing, fantastic, astonishing, marvelous, exceptional; technicolor dream come true

When the character of Maria in *The Sound of Music* was teaching the Von Trapp children to sing, her lovely voice wafted over the Alps, "Let's start at the very beginning, a very good place to start. When you read, you begin with A-B-C, when you sing, you begin with Do-Re-Mi." The same is true in the exploration of bliss. When you answer this invitation though, you begin with 'feel, hear, see' (not to exclude taste and touch, since they are important bliss enhancing senses . . . they just don't fit the rhyme scheme).

Can you go into the experience of opening to bliss, senses fully ablaze? Let's take an inventory with our first ***Bliss Kisses***:

On a scale of 1-10, how fulfilling is your life?

When you awaken every morning, what is your first thought?

Do you wake up smiling or grumbling?

Would you categorize your life as mundane or magical?

Sixties songbird Peggy Lee voiced the musical question, "Is that all there is?" Is that your theme song?

If a movie were made of your life, would it be a comedy, drama, action/adventure flick, horror film, or romance?

Do you live with caution or courage?

When was the last time you took my version of the 'Nestea® Plunge', falling backward into the loving arms of the Universe, trusting that you will be safely held?

If never or not recently, are you willing to do so?

When?

If you knew that in a year from now your life could do a 180 degree turnaround and you would be living your passion, how would you feel in this moment?

Did your answer surprise you?

When facing life change, I envision the trapeze artist performing all kinds of tricks and flights of fancy. Then the next trapeze comes swinging toward her. In that moment, she has a choice: she can remain clinging to the trapeze already in her hands, OR she can stretch her body out, take flight, and grab hold of the one headed her way. That moment in free-fall or free-flight can be terrifying or exhilarating. She knows that the act consists of moving from one trapeze to the next. It wouldn't make for an exciting show if she kept swinging back and forth on the same apparatus.

I know too that I can watch amazed as this highly trained person engages in her art and think, "I could never do that." Frankly, I wouldn't want to. My leaps of faith and yours may look a little different from hers, but they take courage nonetheless. The origin of the word is from French 'coeur' which translates to 'from the heart'. I like the idea that we are heart warriors, taking a stand for the kind of lives we deserve and desire; that's a crusade I can get behind.

Chapter 2

Endless Loop Tape

"Intuition is a spiritual faculty and does not explain, but simply points the way."
—*Florence Scovel Shinn*

One clear intuitive experience arrived in an infinitely life changing form. In early 1986, I was invited to go to what was then the Soviet Union with a group of other teachers, writers, and healers on a citizens' diplomacy mission. My friend Alan Cohen was one of the leaders. The purpose of the trip was to join the hearts of Americans and Russians to melt the hardened attitudes of the Cold War mentality. I was excited as during the trip, which was scheduled October 12—25 of that year, I was to turn 26. What a way to celebrate! I paid my deposit and set about preparing for this awesome event. Shortly afterward, I heard what I describe as The Voice For God, a gender neutral communication that clearly stated, "You are not to go to Russia now. You are to be in Philadelphia."

"Huh?" I responded incredulously. "But it's the trip of a lifetime!"

And again, the Voice insisted.

"But I'll be spending my birthday in Russia—the home of some of my ancestors . . ."

And the Voice patiently reiterated.

"But I don't live in Philadelphia."

The endless loop tape's message continued.

Finally, exasperated, I said, "Look at me, arguing with a disembodied voice. You're not going to give up until I do, right?" I could almost see a knowing nod from the I AM. So I canceled my reservation and put the episode on the back burner.

On October 24th, the day before I was to return from Russia, I traveled, with a group of friends, an hour south of where I lived to hear

Ram Dass speak—in Philadelphia—on the subject of Seva (selfless service, in Sanskrit). During the intermission, my friend Ute Arnold approached me with a curly-haired, red-bearded man who held out his hand to shake mine. "This is Michael Moser," Ute introduced in her soft, German accented voice. "He's going to be coming to your *Love Yourself Playshop* in a few weeks."

I had scheduled to teach at a conference a few weeks hence. Had I gone to Russia, I still would have offered a class there, but it would have been about my trip. As such, it was unlikely that Michael would have been drawn to it. I smiled, greeted him warmly, said I looked forward to seeing him at the conference, and then trotted off to visit with other friends.

At the workshop, Michael sat across from me in the circle and—good student that he was—as I was talking about the importance of eye contact in communication, his vivid blue eyes lasered in. I found myself sliding down in my chair . . . oh my!

Over the months, we developed a stronger connection. And in May of 1987, we were married with our friend Ute, who introduced us, playing the role of 'Best Person'. To this day, I think of Ram Dass as our yenta (matchmaker), and in the three times I have interviewed him over the years, I have told him so.

Michael and I shared adventures over the twelve years we were married. We published *Visions Magazine* from 1988—1998, which focused on wellness and transformation. We adopted our then nearly 5-year-old (now 24-year-old) son. We moved to Florida to start the second regional edition of our magazine. Then in 1992, which I lovingly call 'our year from hell', I had an ectopic pregnancy and nearly died, Michael was diagnosed with Hepatitis C, and we lost our house in Homestead, Florida to Hurricane Andrew. During that period, a sense of knowing that all was well, even in the midst of the challenges, was what sustained me.

We moved back to the Philly area on January 1, 1998, and Michael's condition worsened. Over the next several months, he went in and out of the hospital, racking up 'frequent flier miles' each time we passed through the ER door. His final entry into the ICU while awaiting a liver transplant was on 11/11/98, and I lived there with him over the subsequent five and a half weeks, holding daily dialogues with the Divine. I sometimes called them God-wrestling sessions where I would say, "He's mine and you can't have him."

The response I would receive was, "He's mine and he's on loan to you like everyone else in your life." Again, I sighed and surrendered.

On December 21, 1998, as the life support was turned off, my messenger returned . . . the same Voice that I heard in 1986 now told me to call the seminary and ask to finish what Michael had started. I knew exactly what that meant. Michael had enrolled in The New Seminary to become an interfaith minister—I had casually studied with him. Reading to him, typing his papers when he was too ill to do so, quizzing him and the like, I knew the subject matter well. A few days after his Christmas Eve funeral, I contacted the school and asked to enroll. Welcomed with open arms, I was told that in order to graduate with Michael's class, I needed to complete my two years of study simultaneously, or I could wait until the following year to be ordained. I completed both years' work in five months, with what I called Divine and husbandly intervention, while working full-time as a nursing home social worker. It was part of my healing process. In June of 1999, I walked down the aisle of the Cathedral of St. John the Divine in NYC, carrying with me a photo of Michael, the man who entered my life as companion and guide.

Bliss Kisses

Can you recall a time in your life when intuition whispered in your ear?

Did you heed the call?

If you didn't listen to the soft voice, did it then roar to get your attention?

What happened when you followed the guidance of intuition?

What happened when you didn't?

Chapter 3

As My Own Woman

"Our deepest wishes are whispers of our authentic selves. We must learn to respect them. We must learn to listen."
—Sarah Ban Breathnach

A few years ago, a friend described to me an aunt who lived what seemed to me to be the life of a Bliss Mistress. She was ahead of her time, wearing pants when it was considered unseemly for a woman to do so. She was outspoken, a bit brazen, and—according to my friend—"her own woman." Cosmically coincidentally, her name was Edie too! It got me to thinking about how I choose to live as my own woman. Keeping in mind that there are no absolutes, I remember the wise words of my friend Liora Hill, "I am a work in progress. I am where I am in my process. And where I am in my process is perfect."

My Wo-manifesto

I live full out, regardless of what anyone thinks.
I refuse to dim my light for anyone in order for them to feel comfortable.
I accept all the abundance that the Universe offers.
I forgive myself and others for perceived slights.
I live with compassion both inwardly and outwardly.
I see my own beauty, without the 'yes, but's', and 'if only's', simply . . . as is.
I move with grace, dancing to whatever music I hear.
I sing out with enthusiasm.
I speak my truth.
I welcome Love in all forms.
I refuse to second-guess myself.
I tell the people in my life what they mean to me.
I keep my heart open.

I imagine beyond limitations.
I mirror back the beauty in others I encounter.
I walk barefoot literally and figuratively.
I refrain from 'guilty pleasures' and instead simply call them pleasures.
*I ask for what I want, knowing that I may
not receive **exactly** as I have asked.*
I accept what is for the Highest Good.
I embellish my body with colors, fabrics, and designs that make me feel good.
I move on when a situation warrants it.
I sit with my own feelings, not pushing them away out of fear.
I surrender to 'what is'.
I trust in Divine timing.
I unburden myself of excess baggage.
I live in integrity.
I am genuine and transparent; what you see is what you get.
I am learning to be subtle.
I say 'yes' and 'no' with equal ease.
*I ask for what my work is worth without
stuttering, and I expect to receive it.*
I emotional bungee-jump, enjoying the ride in free-fall.
I stand in my own Truth.
I breathe.

Be insatiable for the kind of life you deserve to live. Take your foot off the brake that keeps your audacious auto from taking you where you want to go. Roll back the stone that keeps you trapped in your cave of solitude. Throw away the jailer's key and push past the door you feel has kept you from being your highest self. I invite you, as my friend singer-songwriter Billy Jonas proclaims in his song "God Is In," to sing and dance with me way past full.

Bliss Kisses

So, what is your personal manifesto?

If you were to live as your own woman or man, how would that be?

Chapter 4

Pissing on the Fire

*"Yet how proud we are, in daring to
look down upon ourselves!"*
—*Elizabeth Barrett Browning*

In conversation with my friend Chris the other day, she tells me that most of her women friends (myself included) are fiery and passionate, with an ability to put themselves out there in the world. I do see myself in that light . . . and yet, far too often I find myself 'pissing on the fire', essentially dousing its warmth and radiance. It takes the form of brushing off compliments as if they are lint fuzzies on my shoulder.

A perfect example occurred just last week. As a freelance journalist, I have begun writing for the website more.com, which is a sister to the glossy magazine *More*. My friends were truly excited for me and offering congratulations. Graciously, I thanked them, and right on the heels of words of gratitude were the obnoxious gremlins, snarling at me. *Yeh, right. If you were such a good writer, you would have Oprah knocking at your door, asking you to write for her magazine, and if you were so talented, you would be making more money for your time* . . . and on it goes until I feel like hurling the yummy Chinese food I had for dinner tonight. Sound familiar?

Just this past week, I was lounging on my orange towel on a Hollywood, Florida beach, enjoying the ocean mist wafting through the refreshing air. Next to me was a group of women who were young enough to be my daughters. I overheard a blond pony-tailed, tie-dye bikini clad 20-something say wistfully, "I'm in such a happy place in my life right now, I'm almost scared. It's so perfect." It was as if she was waiting for the other shoe to drop—for something to go wrong.

In September of 2009, Common Ground Fellowship, an interfaith community of which I have been a part for the past four years, hosted an evening with Dr. Michael Bernard Beckwith and Rickie Byars Beckwith, whom I consider to be a spiritual power couple. He is a dynamically speaking and writing trans-denominational minister and founder of Agape International Spiritual Center in LA. She, besides being the director of the Agape International Choir, is a singer-songwriter with a voice that reaches deep down into the heart and soul of the listener and ain't about to let go. I took on the mantle of what I called 'PR Goddess', doing the public relations and marketing piece for the event. When I first engaged in this process, my initial thoughts were, "Oh goody! Piece of cake!" Little did I know that it wouldn't simply be a light and fluffy assignment. Well, I sorta suspected.

I called the group of us working on the project *Team Transformation*; I knew that we were all being 'worked' by the energy of it and that we would be alchemically transformed as a result. Wow, did that ever bear out! Of course, I can only speak for myself, but my sense is that the others might say something similar. It stretched me in ways that I had never considered. It sharpened my communication skills, since I had to find all manner of creative means to express a similar message. It allowed me the chance to be assertive in asking for what I wanted—to have the seats in the grand, high ceilinged, cathedral setting Tindley Temple venue filled—and they were. It presented me with a test of my visioning/intention setting skills. It gave me the gift of certainty that no matter what, all was/is in Divine Order. Not just faith, but an absolute KNOWING that all was well.

Perhaps one of the greatest gifts was to be smack dab in the middle of an ego-storm. I allowed my buttons to feel pushed each time a media contact didn't jump on-board with enthusiasm to cover the story, each time someone said they wouldn't be there, and each time someone wanted me to do something counter to what I had in mind. What a little brat that ego can be at times! Even more insidious and less blatant was the sense that somehow it fell all on me to fill the seats, which couldn't have been farther from the truth. Within short order, I really understood that this was way bigger than me. It was also way bigger than the mind chatter that Michael Beckwith spoke of that night—the conversation that we are having with our minds when we are out taking a walk. He shared that when intention meets condition, all manner of miracles occur.

As I sat in the pews, I had two competing inclinations. The first was to keep looking at the stage, not wanting to miss a drop of what was going on up there. The second was the pull to witness what was going on all around me: the radiantly beautiful Earth Mother Rickie, resplendent in flowing rainbow garb, belting out waves of love in song form; the celestial choir comprised of folks from different faith communities in PA, NJ, and DE; the clergy from various traditions, sharing their blessings; the musicians carrying us on magic carpets of notes, chords, and drum beat rhythms; and the reaching in and grabbing of the common heart we shared with the words of Michael. THAT was the real story. It was the response of the people singing, dancing, praying, laughing and smiling. THAT'S why we put our hearts and souls into this wondrous event. What these folks will carry out into their daily lives, mattered big time . . . they got it, they truly did. I kept thinking, "We threw this party and look who all showed up!"

Something else jumped out at me in Michael's message when he shared the notion that delay is not denial. A few years ago, I was asked by a magazine to interview Michael. Through Deva Premal and Miten, internationally known kirtan artists who came into my life two years earlier while performing in Philadelphia, I connected with his secretary Maria who excitedly attempted to schedule the interview. When Michael's publisher voted for more mainstream coverage, I felt disappointment and surrendered the interview.

Time passed and I was now sitting on-board the Beckwith event as PR Goddess. *Wisdom Magazine*, one of the publications for which I am a freelance journalist, agreed to have Michael featured in an upcoming issue. It then occurred to me that had the original interview request from a year ago been granted, it would not have held near as high the impact. This interview helped promote an event destined to change the lives of thousands, including myself. The intention was always there, but the conditions had to be right—as Michael said. When he finished signing his last book, I sat with him and shared this story and the one about seed planting 20 years ago that led to my interview of Michael's friend, His Holiness the Dalai Lama. He smiled in recognition, I imagine, at the perfection of those two experiences.

Two interesting things happened on the way home. I was parked at 15th and Catherine, a few blocks from the temple. When I first got out of the car that day, I noticed a penny on the street next to the sidewalk that I didn't pick up. When I got back to the car later it was still there, but it had invited a REALLY good friend . . . a twenty dollar bill! The bill was folded and lying right next to the penny. As I was driving home a little after midnight, I happened upon a sobriety check point. I don't drink alcohol, and if they had stopped me, I would have had to say that I was God-intoxicated. When I mentioned this to a friend afterward, he said he had come up with a new driving citation called DRUID—'DRiving Under the Influence of Deity'. But I was left alone as they were stopping cars on the *other* side of the road. Feeling completely relieved after such a long day, it took me no longer to reach my destination than I planned.

Then today, while at the monthly Common Ground Sunday Sacred Circle, I was sharing my residual feelings with Chris who had been the project manager for the event. I glanced backward at the process of co-creating the evening and still felt a twinge of self-criticism. It brought to mind a sign I saw posted at a time clock where I once worked that proclaimed, "The beatings will continue until morale improves around here." I heard echoes of a conversation with a grad school friend named Alan, who said while we were making dinner in his kitchen one night, "I have an image of you standing over yourself with a whip." Twenty four years later, I still pick it up from time to time.

Chris' sage response was an invitation to put it down. "Are you willing to do that right here and now?" As much as I know I need to do so in order to move forward, sometimes it feels as though that whip is glued to my hand. Never in a million years would I be so critical with someone else. What gives me the right to be that harsh with myself?

Lately I have had dreams that contain violent scenes: terrorists, rape, beatings. Dark imagery that is bewildering for this pacifist to comprehend is being generated in my mind. When I was in the midst of the dreams, I felt like an impartial observer; I simply witnessed. No racing heart or sweating upon awakening. It wasn't until my fully conscious state kicked in to high gear that my distress followed suit. These symbols don't appear randomly—there is a reason why someone like me has dreams with images that she wouldn't normally consider during the day. One thought is that each component of a dream is also part of the dreamer. As I write this chapter, I see the correlation. I have been terrorizing myself and violating myself with my own hyper-critical and deprecating thoughts.

I wish I could say that I am completely free of those toxic judgments I hold against myself for not quite matching up to my own expectations. The process of writing this book brings with it the opportunity to heal as part of the journey of re-awakening. What I ask of myself only is that I allow the fire to burst forth in all its glory, unafraid that it might burn me or someone else. The element can be either constructive or destructive, depending on intent. I choose to burn brightly without hiding my light under the proverbial bushel.

Bliss Kisses

What *positively* incendiary ideas do you have within you ready to burst forth into the world?

Can you think of ways in which you douse the fires of your own ideas and passions?

In what ways are you beating yourself?

Are you willing to put down the implements with which you may terrorize yourself?

Chapter 5

Fifth Chakra Folly

"The most important thing in communication is hearing what isn't being said."
—Peter Drucker

As I'm writing this article, I can hear commentary from one of my friends echoing in my sore ears. "You're the only person I know who can turn a physical ailment into a story to share," I hear with a bit of a silly smirk across his face, knowing that I'm going to do it anyway. That's because there's a story for everything, and we don't have to look far to find it. In my case, it found me.

While the true timing may be more like years or my entire life, for the past few months in particular, I've noted my loving friends and family reminding me to slow down, stop doing, and just BE. At the mere thought of inactivity, fear gripped me. I shrugged it off and kept on running. From what, I wasn't quite sure at the time. Over the past few days, I've had the opportunity and necessity to discover at least a partial truth.

It began a little more than a week ago with a slight sore throat and headache. Deciding I just needed to take a little time off, I defined the solution as an hour or so of meditation or even a yoga class. However, as additional events on my already full calendar, they admittedly still embodied 'doing' rather than simply BE-ing. And by the next day, the minor inconvenience turned into a roaring flame in my throat. Combine that with a history of asthma, bronchitis, and pneumonia—and my lungs began to shut down for business. In an effort to jump start my vocal chords, every cough instead strained them. We're not just talking 'sotto voce', but what I described as Minnie-Mouse-on-helium, to which my friend Greg commented, "Oh, a Disney cold."

It sure felt like Minnie, Mickey, Goofy, Pluto, Snow White, all seven dwarfs, and even the spirit of Walt himself were doing a boogaloo in my respiratory system. "Heigh-ho, Heigh-ho, it's off to work we go," they sang while swinging their little pickaxes and shovels. At pivotal moments, such as trying to communicate with patients and coworkers, or at dinner with friends the other night, I could manage nothing more than a squeak. Frustrating at first, then frightening. I identify myself as a communicator, with speech being my primary source—it's one way I provide income and also how I stay connected to the world around me. I could feel a sense of panic beginning to build. What if I'm shut down for days or weeks?

That night, sleep eluded me as the coughing began to take on a baby seal quality. In baby seals, the high pitched 'barking' is kinda cute. In me, it just wasn't.

I awoke the next morning in full blown terror, as if my throat had closed completely. Swallowing and breathing had been prior apparent luxuries. An early morning phone call to my friends Harmony and Glenda drew me away from the darkness of my fears and into the light of healing.

It occurred to me that some of this was a connection to the way in which my husband Michael had passed seven years earlier. He had been intubated after falling into a coma. The sense of drowning and suffocating that I felt may have been what he experienced. This time of year is the anniversary of his death. Sleep eluded me then as well, and I functioned on 2—3 hours' worth each night while curled up on the waiting room couch if available, or a chair if not. I had promised myself that this year would be different; I had 'moved on' and dealt with the loss.

I've learned that grief can be tricky in stepping forward and then backing off, hiding for a bit, and then appearing right before our eyes the next moment. I no longer identify myself by the loss, but by the strengths and wisdom I have received as its gifts. Even the breathing difficulties were echoed by one of the friends with whom I had dinner this week. She experienced a traumatic loss earlier this year and now has moments of challenge with breathing.

According to author and teacher Anodea Judith, in an interview I conducted with her for the September 2008 issue of *Wisdom Magazine:*

> *The Sanskrit word [chakra] means 'wheel', but my personal definition is that it is a center of organization; a place that organizes, just like your kitchen organizes your food, for the reception, assimilation and the expression of life force energy on different levels. Right now you are hearing my words, so you are receiving my words. You are assimilating them and turning them into meaning in your own mind and you are responding. You will say something to me or later you will tell someone something you learned. That's your expression. We do this with life, love, sound and breath. They are gateways between the inner and outer world through which we have this exchange of life force energy.*

The Fifth chakra, or throat chakra, relates to personal expression and our inner voice of wisdom—a guide to what is 'so'. It is all about communication and speaking our truth. It also extends to the physiological structures of lungs, esophagus, vocal cords, and sense of hearing. Whaddya' know?

From the website nothingbutyoga.com:

> *The emotion for the 5th chakra is faith and understanding. Because the 5th chakra is located in the throat and governs higher communication, speaking, hearing and listening, it helps us to understand our inner truth and convey it with our voice to the outside world. The sense for the 5th chakra is hearing. Chanting, singing, speaking, reading aloud are all good for the 5th chakra. The vibrations of all these things affect the body down to the cellular level.*

All of this proves a perfect reflection of the processes in my life at the moment. In an effort to bring into my life all that I desire, I am running myself ragged and running away from 'nothing'. In wanting to fill perceived empty spaces and empty moments with SOMETHING, I've been doing anything to avoid feeling NOTHING.

In addition to the psycho-spiritual exploration, I knuckled under and visited my friendly physician's assistant, who put me on a low dose of antibiotics to cool the fire in my throat and lungs. I also received a prescription for a heavy-duty cough suppressant with codeine. Providing a dual benefit, I slept for the first time in weeks. Somehow I managed to get to work for a few hours this morning to 'be responsible' and facilitate a family therapy session. I also completed two admission assessments and two discharge plans for patients before I stumbled home to bed, where I once again entered deep and almost refreshing sleep. I'd like to note here that when prescriptions instructions indicate not to operate equipment or drive, they mean it. Guardian angels must have driven the car home. I know I didn't.

In the time I spent not speaking, but rather listening to others and my own inner voice, something else occurred to me in the form of a valuable relationship lesson: everybody plays by their own rules. As much as I would like to think (as does everyone) that my rules work, they might not for someone else. Expecting another person—be it a child, friend or partner—to play by my rules only sets us both up for disappointment and frustration. It's about communication, flexibility, and negotiation. Fifth chakra lesson if ever there was one.

So I am still breathing and not speaking as I save my voice for teaching a workshop tomorrow. Whispering when necessary. No more fear. The experience gave me insight into how some of my patients may be feeling when they are gripped with what seems like unreasonable terror that no amount of reassurance can calm.

I am also attempting more self compassion, which is a lesson brought home literally in the form of the loving gift of a beautiful Kwan Yin statue I received this week. She is the Chinese Goddess of Compassion. When she died, she had the opportunity to enter Nirvana. At the pivotal moment, hearing the cries of the suffering still on the Earth plane, she turned back and chose to remain here until all are free from suffering. Statues of Kwan Yin show her in flowing robes, barefoot, and graceful in appearance. She is said to embody perfect compassion, unconditional love, and deep empathy. I strive to follow her example, but first I have to be open to the guidance. Om Shanti and deep silent peace to you all.

Bliss Kisses

In what ways have you neglected your well-being?

What have the consequences been?

How can you be more compassionate with yourself?

Was there a time when you didn't 'speak your truth'?

Do you need to take more time in silence to listen to the inner voice?

Chapter 6

A Love Letter to Yourself

"To love oneself is the beginning of a life-long romance."
—*Oscar Wilde*

Within a breath after (and maybe even before) the holiday decorations emptied from store shelves, they were replaced with vividly hued red and pink items that heralded another gift giving and card offering event . . . Valentine's Day. For many, it is a reminder of loved ones lost.

I remember the Valentine's Days when my husband was alive that would begin with cards and gifts hidden under the bed which we would reach under our respective sides to retrieve. Simple things, with creative sentiments, that would allow us to sink into the playfulness that hallmarked our relationship. December 2008 marked the 10th anniversary of his passing. While I honor our relationship as it existed then, I am no longer married to him or the past that we shared. It now lives on as an incorporated part of all that I am.

In that spirit, I celebrate each day as a Valentine's Day in which I honor the love that is abundant in every relationship in my life . . . friends and lovers, family members, co-workers, and casual acquaintances I pass on the street.

It is so much easier to express love to these 'others' than it is to ourselves, yet I have discovered that I cannot truly and fully offer to anyone else what I do not feel for myself. To do so otherwise rings hollow. Over the years, I have engaged in a practice that I invite you to indulge in as well: a love letter to yourself.

Imagine, if you will, that someone you love dearly is writing you the most exquisite creation coming straight from the heart. As we age, we sometimes come face-to-face with 'shoulda, woulda, coulda' regrets; we look at our bodies and recall a time when they may have been leaner or more flexible and could do more things than they can now. One of my favorite lines comes from Pete Seeger, "How do I know that my youth is all spent? My get up and go has got up and went. But in spite of it all, I'm able to grin, when I think of the places my get up has been."

But I digress . . . back to the letter.

Pick out a beautiful card or a piece of stationary. Use a lovely color ink and let flow from your pen words both eloquent and affirming. What would send you swooning? What would have you feel cherished and treasured? You can write about your physical attributes—choose one thing you like when you gaze into the mirror. Offer a tribute to your generous spirit, your open heart, your creativity, or even your gardening skills. Then, seal it in an envelope and give it to a friend to mail you in a few weeks or at a time when you may have forgotten that you had written it. It will show up in your mailbox as a delightful surprise. Remember, guys, this is not just an exercise for the women. Men need affirmation too.

So, as we appreciate those we love and cherish, make sure to honor the lover in the mirror.

Bliss Kisses

How can you offer yourself the kind of love that you easily give to others?

What limiting thoughts might put blocks to self adoration?

Would you want to be married to you?

Chapter 7

The Servant of the Creation

"The world is but a canvas to the imagination."
—*Henry David Thoreau*

I am a voracious reader; I come by it genetically and by inclination. My favorite genres focus on transformation, spirituality, sexuality, sci-fi, relationships, and the lyrically (and sometimes quirkily) poetic. A few years ago I picked up a book that contained some of the above. Within short order, this travelogue of the heart that took the writer on a one year journey to Italy, India, and Indonesia became a worldwide best seller. *Eat, Pray, Love* was penned by author Elizabeth Gilbert. Immediately attracted to the familiar, conversational style with which she draws the reader, I felt as if I was being carried along for the ride without need for passport or inoculation.

    I attended a presentation that Liz offered in New Hope, PA. The topic touched me to my core, since it was as if she and I were sitting face-to-face exploring the nature of creativity. She waxed both philosophical and practical about the ways in which our ideas come. One particular concept that latched hold was that while those of us who write, sing, dance, paint, draw, and design may believe that it is *we* who are creating, we are really the *servants* of the creation. Our artistry comes through us and not from us. I often state emphatically that "my writing writes me." It uses me as a vehicle and voice to find its expression in the world. In spiritual terms, I sometimes say that I am God's Typist, and as 13th century 'ecstatic' Sufi poet Rumi refers to it—a "hollow reed."

    I find inspiration EVERYWHERE! It can be while cleaning a closet, sweating at the gym, in conversation with a friend, driving on a highway, reading someone else's words, writing my own, floating deep in dreamland, or meditating. It arrives in unexpected ways and from unanticipated sources. I welcome it from wherever it has traveled to make its way to my door. According to wikipedia, "Inspiration refers to an unconscious burst of creativity in a literary, musical, or other artistic endeavor. Literally, the word means 'breathed upon'." I like the idea of being breathed by the Divine.

I was listening to the radio in the car last week and Rod Stewart burst forth with "Every Picture Tells A Story." He grabbed me and took me on his worldwide whirlwind that was far grittier and less poetic than Liz's trip, but along I went. It occurred to me that not only does every picture tell a story, but every story paints a word picture. Although I used to claim that I wasn't an artist, I can now retract that statement. As a writer, I have been told by readers that I do indeed paint word pictures into which they can step, dance, drift, or dream.

When I set fingers to keyboard, I can imagine—eyes closed of course—that I am holding in my hand the wisp of a paintbrush. Sometimes dipping it into subtle colors, I more often plunge it into outrageous-jumping-up-and-down-look-at-me vibrant hues that splash across the paper begging to soak them up. *Whew!* Just typing those words gives me an intake of breath and causes butterflies to dance within . . .

So, I ask you:

Bliss Kisses

What creative force within you is calling out to be recognized?

Have you answered the call or told it nobody's home?

How have you squelched your creativity?

How have you celebrated it?

Chapter 8

Everything I Need To Know, I Learned at Cuddle Party

"A hug is like a boomerang. You get it back right away."
—*Bill Keane*

There are times when the Universe issues an irresistible invitation, and we are helpless to do anything but respond. Mine came in the form of a posting on a website called *By Region* on which events are listed by region of the country, hence the name. With the clever moniker Cuddle Party™, one such event enticed this insatiable cuddler to travel two hours northward to a 5th floor walk-up in Manhattan—the home of Reid Mihalko and Marcia Baczynski. Relationship coaches and educators, they are the creators of the workshop born on February 29, 2004 that is now a worldwide phenomenon. Considering New York City is not known as a bastion of snuggly souls, I was pleasantly surprised when, in the company of the eighteen attendees, I felt very much at home.

Cuddle Party is a 3 ½ hour experiential workshop for adults age 18 and over that focuses on communication, boundary setting, relationships, intimacy, self-esteem, community building, and safe, nurturing, nonsexual touch. It is attended by folks dressed in all manner of fun and colorful pajamas. During the first forty minutes or so, "The Welcome Circle" is formed, creating a safe space for what follows: two hours or so of 'freestyle cuddling' taking the form of spooning, snuggling, massaging, and nuzzling—all with verbal consent of each participant. I think of it as grownup Twister® in which one person may be massaging your shoulders while you are working on someone else's feet and someone else is spooned up next to them. Although the touch component of the workshop gets the lion's share of attention, Cuddle Party is about far more than that. Relationships have grown, self-esteem has been enhanced, body image has been accepted, communication has been improved, new friendships have been formed, and emotional challenges have been faced. It isn't therapy, but it does seem to have therapeutic value.

I left the event filled to overflowing with Oxytocin, known as the 'cuddle hormone', which is also secreted when mothers nurse and helps them bond with their babies. By the time I left, I knew two things:

1. I wanted to bring Cuddle Party to Philadelphia (and so Reid came down twice that summer to offer the workshop).

2. I felt moved to become a certified Cuddle Party facilitator.

In September of the same year, I trekked back to New York and spent the weekend in the company of some of the most talented, creative, and genuinely affectionate people on the planet. Much of the training's content allowed me to explore my co-dependence, in addition to what was serving me well in my life and relationships.

I gave myself permission to ask the question, "How's the listening in the room?" This relates to the idea that in any conversation, there are really several conversations going on at once: the immediate dialog, the thought inside your head about how you might respond to what the other person is saying, and the wonder of how the other person might respond to you. When the listening is satisfactory, each person is fully present with the other. I also learned about the concept of 'coming clean' and gave myself permission to share whatever I might have been withholding—the good, the bad, and the ugly.

At that point, I had been a workshop facilitator for at least 25 years and yet, as I sat with Reid and Marcia, I found myself adding powerful 'portable life skills' to my teaching tool kit.

I referred to my first three practice Cuddle Parties as my 'training wheel parties', since in many ways, I felt like a little kid on a bike (which is a metaphor that is used in a different way during the didactic part of the workshop). When the time came to facilitate the first, I was actually nervous. That is an unaccustomed feeling for this verbal veteran. All of my *what if enough people don't show up for it to count* thoughts threatened to scoop me up and run away with me. There is a minimum number required for the parties, and feedback forms are completed by attendees. Each time I called Reid for support in advance, he talked me through stage fright. His words, "Darlin', the event will go as the event will go," were a rallying cry and—of course—he was on target.

Yes, there were plenty of cuddlers present who enjoyed the experience. With their support, I made it to the next steps in the certification process and fulfilled the requirements. In a final phone call from Reid and the first certified facilitator, Len Daley, I heard the words, "By the power vested in us . . . by no one but ourselves . . . we now declare you Cuddle Party Facilitator #27!" I literally jumped up and down as if on a pogo stick, hooting and hollering. The accomplishment was right up there with completing grad school and being ordained as an interfaith minister.

With that, I was off and running and scheduling Cuddle Parties by inviting willing huggers, snugglers, cuddlers, spooners, and nuzzlers. Each time, I learned something new from the participants about trust, surrender, and safely stretching comfort zones. Since that time, I figure I have offered around 150 Cuddle Parties. When I consider how many people have attended and then left to spread the love they experienced, I am deeply gratified.

As a PR Goddess, I was in my glory, letting the media know about the workshop that had been so positively life changing. I also held what is referred to as 'media friendly Cuddle Parties', in which the press is invited to observe and even participate, as long as they agree to the *Rules of Cuddling:*

1. *Pajamas stay on the whole time.*
2. *You don't have to cuddle anyone at a Cuddle Party ever.*
3. *You must ask permission and receive a verbal YES before you touch anyone.*
4. *If you're a yes, say YES; if you're a no, say NO.*
5. *If you're a maybe, say NO.*
6. *You are encouraged to change your mind.*
7. *Respect your relationship boundaries and communicate with your partner.*
8. *Get your Cuddle Party Facilitator or Cuddle Assistant if you have a question or concern or need assistance with anything during the Cuddle Party.*
9. *Tears and laughter are both welcome.*
10. *Respect people's privacy when sharing about Cuddle Parties.*
11. *Keep the cuddle space tidy. (Snacks are served, which explains this rule.)*

I have enjoyed hosting members of the press from The Philadelphia Inquirer, Fox 29 News, and CBS 3 Philadelphia in attendance over the past few years. Since Cuddle Party is considered a bit left of center for main stream media, it was a novelty and curiosity. And at times, it was the brunt of lewd and lascivious attention. As much as I attempted to communicate that it was indeed a nonsexual event—in which clothing stays on, hands remain on top of the clothing, and there is no touch with the intent to arouse—there have been those who felt it was a cover for an orgy. This couldn't be further from the truth.

After one of the newscasts, which was picked up by *Good Morning Yahoo*, comedic pundit Stephen Colbert lampooned the event on April 29, 2008. Slightly mortified by the "Wag of the Finger" and Colbert's reference to the parties as something like an orgy for the socially inept, I was assured once again by Reid that any publicity was good publicity. I then brazenly invited Mr. Colbert to bring his pajama-clad butt to one of my Cuddle Parties so he would be able to speak from direct experience. I have yet to hear from him, but a cuddly space awaits in just his shape and size at any of them.

Although Cuddle Party is embraced (no pun intended) by a growing number of people worldwide, there are some who are still leery. I hear their comments of it being "icky" and wonderment of who would want to cuddle with strangers. I cannot help but reply with the query, "Wasn't everyone you know and love *now* once a stranger?"

There have also been insinuations that only weird, lonely, socially awkward people would attend. I can state with all certainty that people who come to Cuddle Party would not be discernible from those you see waiting in a supermarket check out line, sitting at an adjacent table at a five star restaurant, or riding next to you on a train. Teachers, doctors, students, Marines, a marine biologist, yoga instructors, massage therapists, coaches, clergy, homemakers, parents, grandparents, teachers, engineers, computer techs, and attorneys have all been guests at my Cuddle Parties.

People from various cultures, spiritual beliefs, body size, and ability have participated. You need not be in relationship to attend. Couples and individuals as young as 18 and as old as 80 (and beyond) have joined us in the 'puppy pile'.

For many people, touch has been limited, non-existent, sexual, or abusive. At Cuddle Party, it is plentiful, safe, consensual, and nurturing. One of my greatest joys is observing how people, who may have entered the room feeling timid, float out on an Oxytocin high to share their experiences with others in their lives. Many are 'frequent cuddlers' who return time after time to enjoy healthy touch with their family of choice. I have been gratified to witness that trauma survivors have learned that they can be in charge of setting healthy touch boundaries.

Although Cuddle Party is not a dating service and not about 'hooking up', I have been pleased to see relationships begin as a result of people meeting there. One beautiful story emerged when a man who had attended for years stopped coming to them after meeting a woman with whom he developed a loving relationship—one that he credits the workshop with helping him grow. They married, inviting me to participate in the ceremony, and now have a delightful son who I would bet is quite cuddly himself.

I was fortunate to have been raised in an environment in which I was offered love in physical form as well as verbal. When I became certified, I told my parents that they had raised me to be a Cuddle Party facilitator. My mother has said that she would love to attend, but wouldn't be able to get down on the floor to snuggle, since she couldn't get back up. I assured her that people would gladly come to her. Sadly, she never had the chance to be there, but I sense her presence nonetheless in the 'puppy pile'.

Each day, I bless Reid and Marcia for creating this workshop that allows me to "come to work dressed in pj's, get paid to touch and be touched . . . and it's legal."

Cuddle On!

Bliss Kisses

What role has touch played in your life?

What comes to mind when you hear the words cuddle, snuggle, and hug?

What are your personal boundaries when it comes to touch?

Chapter 9

And the Year Has Just Begun

"Year's end is neither an end nor a beginning but a going on, with all the wisdom that experience can instill in us."
—Hal Borland

New Year's weekend 2004 into 2005, I began a ritual that I want to continue for the rest of this earthly incarnation—and maybe beyond. It was an out of the ordinary weekend in many ways: a retreat to a beautiful bay front home at the Jersey shore attended by kindred spirits who danced, sang, drummed, laughed, cooked, and ate together. Led by phenomenal Philly-based performing artist and teacher Ron Kravitz, the weekend was a transformative time for me and I daresay for the others there too.

At midnight, we went outside and howled at the moon overlooking the bay. The weather was unusual for this part of the country too, as on New Year's Day we did yoga on the beach in 70 degree temps. After the practice, I took a solitary walk at water's edge and felt, as I occasionally do, a bit sorry for myself. Facing challenges, I saw no way beyond them at that moment. In a flash, I said to myself, "Snap out of it, woman! Let's make a list of all of the loving souls you have drawn into your life in 2004 and all of the beyond-belief experiences you have had." And so I did. With each name, experience, and step, I felt lighter physically and emotionally.

As the end of 2008 approached, I found myself once again meandering into that practice. I figure I have met thousands of people when I consider the following: those I have interviewed for various publications, those I have married in my role of interfaith minister and their families and friends, those with whom I have attended workshops and classes, and those who have participated in workshops I have taught. Imagine how many people I have snuggled while facilitating Cuddle

Party workshops who have gone on to 'spread the luv' to others. And this doesn't even take into consideration the people with whom I have made a heart connection as a result of another friend's introduction; I am particularly grateful for those matchmaking encounters. I also think about the serendipitous, cosmically coincidental meetings when people show up unexpectedly.

When I look at the list of 2008 experiences, I grin from ear to ear. I had the blessing of living a 20-year journalistic dream of interviewing the Dalai Lama, began hosting my own internet radio show, and I traveled to California to visit friends—was that ever an amazing adventure! As you are now one of my connections, I would like to share the experience with you.

I had traveled cross-country to San Francisco to attend a Cuddle Party facilitator reunion and be with many pajama-clad wonders who teach others how to be authentic in giving and receiving nurturing touch without condition. The experience allowed me to enjoy time with my friend Jaz, whose live and in person warmth and love I hadn't had in awhile.

It was a whirlwind of pure experience. I made a trip to Café Gratitude, indulged in raw food heaven, found a wild and wonderfully purple cotton jacket at Goodwill, and went to a costume party. Steppin' out in a new black silk and lace bustier (my first, but likely not my last), I skipped down the street holding hands with friends and hearing the 1960's anthem written by John Phillips of the Mamas and Papas ringing in my ears: "If you're going to San Francisco, be sure to wear some flowers in your hair." Corny, but true. I met the 'spiritual cowgirl' red-ilicious Sera Beak who wrote *The Red Book,* and I was inspired by this red-volutionary whose work is nothing short of Divine sustenance. I did leave a piece of my heart in San Francisco.

The last night in the city, before winging Eastward, I found myself with friends in a hot tub (more like a cement pond with bubbling water) surrounded by tall bamboo, overlooking the San Francisco Bay, under a full moon. "Could life get much better than this?" I mused aloud to Reid Mihalko who, along with Marcia Baczynski, had created Cuddle Party.

His broadly grinning response was, "This is your birthright, Babe! You get to have this." He really does talk like that.

I invite you to find a way to honor everything that you have done in the past 12 months and all the wondrous people with whom you have crossed paths—folks who you may not even have known existed at this time last year. I encourage you to open your hearts to all the people you have yet to meet who are waiting on the other side of the threshold between last year and this one.

Wishing you a brand new year filled with everything your heart desires, as you leave behind in the previous year anything that no longer serves.

Bliss Kisses

How do you cross thresholds from one year to the next?

List the people you now know who weren't even on your radar screen when the year began.

What do you wish to leave behind?

What do you wish to attract?

Chapter 10

Lila

"You can discover more about a person in an hour of play than in a year of conversation."
—*Plato*

One of my favorite play-buddies is my friend Peter. With him, I have the wondrous experience of 'lila' (pronounced lee-la), translated in the Hindu tradition as 'play'. He and I have been teaching together for close to seven years at this writing. It's hard to imagine that two people in their 50's can earn part of our living by teaching kids in grown-up suits how to just have fun. By most people's observation, neither of us look our age. It could be because on the inside, we just aren't—like all of you, we are ageless.

A few years ago, we were invited to offer our workshop entitled *Happiness Is Just the Icing, Joy Is the Cake* at a conference for early childhood educators. Peter happens to fit that category as his *Music Experience For Young Children* travels to daycare centers and preschools singing, dancing, drumming and reading with little ones. He is also a singer-songwriter who performs in concert. I joke with him that his groupies are usually under four years old and under four feet tall. That's what keeps this father of five—whose young'uns range in age from a bit over one year or so into the thirties—so youthful. In my case, good genes play a role. Or maybe attitude IS everything.

I eagerly anticipated the opportunity to see just how free and open these teachers who work with munchkins from two to four years old could be, and I was delighted to discover the extent this afternoon. But first I had to fulfill my more 'serious' obligation at my full-time salary-and-benefits gig as a social worker in a psychiatric hospital. I went in this morning, handled details of discharge for a few patients, and completed a couple's counseling session before heading out the door to the presentation.

Checking the address, I thought I knew where I was going, only to find that I wasn't quite as certain as initially imagined. I kept driving in circles, a bit concerned about being late. Breathing, I asked the AGS (Angelic Guidance System) and a gentleman at the local post office who may indeed have been an angel himself. I got back on track and pulled into the parking lot, hyperventilating a bit as I hauled the bag of handouts and props toward the building. It wasn't too terribly heavy, because some of the items were the feathers I give out at all of my workshops as a reminder to participants to lighten up, telling them that it can be used to "tickle your fancy, or whatever else you have in mind."

Just then, I was halted in my tracks at the sight of another reminder to lighten up and just play. It was an iridescently glowing green plastic child with the word 'SLOW' written across him. With a deep breath, smile, and pause, I entered the building.

For two hours, sixteen participants laughed, cried, shared, danced, sang, listened to, and supported each other through pure play. We invited them at the onset to fully engage themselves in the process, telling them that life is like the hokey pokey—it's more fun if you put your whole self in. The afternoon flowed effortlessly, as does anything you love as much as we love doing this work. Row-row-row your boat, side by side with Ella Fitzgerald belting out, "It don't mean a thing if you ain't got that swing." Peter encouraged us to trying 'scatting' along with her, and he taught us a silly participatory song called "Tootie Tot" that involved "thumbs up, elbows back, feet apart, knees together, bottoms up, tongues out, and eyes closed." Got it? He was looking forward to challenging 800 or so participants at a larger conference later that month to join in. Heck, it could be the start of a revolution.

When was the last time you really allowed yourself to engage in 'lila' while not in the presence of a chronological child? So many of us have restrictions on when and in whose company play is acceptable. It's the recriminating voice in our heads; as my friend Michael Buck refers to it, it's the 'drunken monkey'—the inner critic that wags its finger at us, reminding us not be frivolous or waste time. Play is as nourishing for our souls as food is for our bodies. Without it, we shrivel up inside and age rapidly on the outside.

Most of the seniors I know are phenomenal role models for vibrancy because they haven't forgotten how to play. My mom and Peter's mom are among them. My friends Gary and Denny lead Spirit Dance gatherings and are in that ageless fold. My Aunt Kate, who died when I was in college, was an amazing role model for enlightened lila. My last clear memory of her was on New Year's Day circa 1980. Friends and I had gone to her apartment to warm up after nearly freezing while watching the Philadelphia grand tradition Mummers Parade. When we walked in, there was this 80-something year old woman in a skirt, blouse, and stocking feet, all out performing the Mummers strut in front of the television as she enjoyed the parade.

What would it take for you to step out of your comfort zones and just dive in heart-first? My personal goal is to leave the drunken monkey at home munching on bananas while I dance out into the world, "true colors shining through," as sings Cindy Lauper, the sometimes kool-aid hair colored poster child of a girl just wantin' to have fun.

Bliss Kisses

What technicolor thing have you always wanted to do?

How can you be more filled with the spirit of lila?

Who are your role models that entice you to play?

Wouldn't it be cool to be that for someone else?

Chapter 11

Once Wild

"Invent your life over if it doesn't feel juicy."
—SARK

Sometime a few years ago, I found an object that I keep in my car to remind me of who I am. It is a faerie in flight with the words of Isadora Duncan inscribed on it: "You were once wild here. Don't let them tame you." She hangs from my rear view mirror lest I am tempted to forget. It caught my attention today on the drive in to work. "What does it mean to be wild?" I mused. Different things to different people, obviously.

Lately, I have called into my life folks who walk a bit of a different path because they are unwilling to be tamed. They dance their passions in a manner that may raise eyebrows, but they have become my role models for going toward a full, rich, juicy life. They range from a movie producer and an astrologer to a man stepping out of his suit-and-tie business attire into purple and blue yoga wrap pants—as he allows his inner healer to come out and play. They include folks like tantra teachers and spiritual mediums, as well as poets and yoga instructors. There is a person who recognizes and honors his true self regardless of form and appearance, putting a smile on my face on Valentine's Day a few years back, and another who stretched his own comfort zones (and mine) this past weekend. There are authors who run the gamut of intellectual and spiritual shares from a book on manifesting your heart's desires to one on recognizing transcendent sexual experiences, and yet another on acknowledging both the Divine and human Beloved. There are too many more to mention, but know that I honor all of them.

Although it may not seem possible to believe, once upon a time I was hesitant and filled with fear. I was timid, like a deer caught in the headlights when it came to making decisions, and according to my husband, "an emotional contortionist who would bend over backward to please people." What changed all of that was the need to rise to the occasion when he became ill. I had to quickly strip off the shroud of lingering self-doubt. I didn't have the luxury of a negative thought. And once that became second nature, I was able to relax into the experience. With each new friendship, I felt nourished, absorbing the love and the inspiration that they shared. I saw that it was possible to live my dreams fully and freely without, as Michael was fond of saying, "Looking over your shoulder to see if the propriety police were watching you." I found out that they really weren't even in the neighborhood, let alone focusing their attention on what I was up to.

Over the past few years, the desire to stretch even further was kindled within me. Multiple opportunities to 'be my bliss' present themselves daily, mostly because I invite them in. Lately, I have been questioning the fears that used to plague me and wonder about their origin. I had a conversation with my mother during which I told her that even at 47, I still valued their approval. Speaking with her, I quoted something I recall my parents telling me as I was growing up: "Don't do anything we'd be ashamed of," juxtaposed with, "Anything you do will be good enough."

She said in surprise, "We never told you not to do anything we would be ashamed of, but rather not to do anything you would be ashamed of."

All these years, I had been living with a misunderstood version and acted as if my parents should be the barometer of the validity and worthiness of my choices. *Whoa!* Big revelation there. If I can face the woman in the mirror each day and know that I am in integrity with my decisions, then I am living that innocence rather than shame. As a woman, I have struggled with this dichotomy of wanting to revel in my strengths and 'goddess energy' and simultaneously fearing it, all the while projecting that fear onto men I have drawn into my life. Naturally, the more comfortable I am with the energy, the more at ease they will be with it.

This past weekend, at a workshop in Maryland, I participated in a puja (a Hindu ritual that honors the Divine in each being present) and found myself face-to-face and heart-to-heart with a few men in the circle. Afterward, I commented that no one seemed overwhelmed and no one's head exploded in the midst of so much Shakti (Divine feminine) energy. Later that evening, one man told me he welcomed powerful women into his life, and I felt honored by his expression of that statement.

My friend, Naila Francis, sent this poem today that 'wrote her', and I share it with you here as it resonates with my own experience of living wildly and with passion:

> *I vibrate to the rhythm of joy*
> *Gladly accepting its sublime invitation to dance*
> *Twirling with the stars, spinning on the sun's golden beams*
> *Carrying laughter in my belly that rises up in exultation*
> *Triumphantly giddy in unleashing its fullness on the world*
> *Below, I tread on fields of endless possibility*
> *Above, the angels soar, all glitter and glory, in delight at my effervescence*
> *I vibrate to the rhythm of joy*
> *That casts my world in brilliant incandescence*
> *And I am bold in drawing beauty to my heart*
> *In weaving dreams so deliciously outrageous*
> *I taste their unfolding, like a sweetness on my tongue*
> *Yes, joy, joy and more joy*
> *I am soaking in it*
> *Reveling in it*
> *Expanding in its powerful presence*
> *Vibrating to the rhythm*
> *That is God expressing pure pleasure*
> *In the perfection of His creation*

Like Naila, I too invite you to drink in the nectar of your own beautiful, wild self as you live your passion and purpose.

Bliss Kisses

In what ways could you be a little wilder?

Can you think of times in your life when you misheard or misunderstood something that was said to you, acting as if that was the truth?

Can you think of times in your life when you heard and understood something said to you that did not internally resonate, but you still accepted it as the truth—not allowing your own truth in?

Are you willing to step forward into your own power without being overpowering?

Is it time to live a wondergasmic life?

Chapter 12

Plugged into Our Source

"Spirit is an invisible force made visible in all life."
—*Maya Angelou*

Recently I had a revelation by way of a strand of wiring, a battery, and a piece of electronic circuitry that provides education, entertainment, and a portion of my right livelihood, which you are now reading. I was sitting at my trusty laptop computer, busily typing an article, and noticed that the screen went dim. While I know there are times my eyes experience fatigue from hours of concentration without a break, this was something entirely different. I observed that the plug which connects the computer to the battery was slightly dislodged.

The moment I fit it back into its little outlet . . . *ta-da* . . . the screen was once again illuminated. So simple a fix, carrying with it so profound a message. Just as the computer needed to be connected to its power source in order to function at an optimum level, so too do we need to be tapped into our Source. You might call it God, Goddess, Spirit, Creator, Divine, Higher Power, the Universe, or any number of other names. It matters not how you refer to it.

Many is the day when I have to remind myself to check my connection, particularly when I am feeling overwhelmed, angry, or frustrated. I start the process I reference as 'running on adrenalin and fumes'. Not only have I felt physically fatigued and emotionally drained, I've also felt spiritually empty. My ability to handle everyday life dips down into the red zone. My compassion meter runs a quart low, and I am scraping the bottom of the barrel for ideas and energy. You get the picture.

When the link is secure, so too am I—the love flows unimpeded. I feel a sense of Oneness with all that is, and almost nothing rattles me. At that level, I am not disturbing my own peace, ruffling my own feathers, or pulling the rug straight out from under my own self.

Another issue I faced is one that centers around asking and then receiving what I have asked for. We should all have such a problem. I am a firm knower (not just believer) that when I set intention, it usually occurs—either as I have requested or something even more blow-me-out-of-the-water amazing than I could have imagined. What I have been visioning is writing and speaking full-time. In the past few months, opportunities and offers have been streaming in. New friends and collaborators show up By Divine Design, which is the name of my business. The title came to me in a dream, and when I asked what those words meant, The Voice said, "You'll know."

For the past 20 years I have been a journalist, interviewing many of the movers and shakers in the transformational fields. I have seen myself on the 'big stage', much like them, and I am certain that is part of my purpose and certainly my passion. Lately I have even been invited to speak and to be interviewed on the same radio programs. And yet . . . there is still this 'agnoxious' (a conjunction of the words *aggravating* and *obnoxious*) voice yammering at me . . . about worthiness. As one radio host said to me when I acknowledged that I was among lofty company, "You're a star too." My friend Peggy Tileston promised to call me on it anytime I was tempted to hide my light under a bushel. In an interview this past week with Candy Danzis, who refers to herself as 'The Mainstream Mystic', she reminded me that in order for Spirit to use me to shine through, I need to make myself available to allow it. Shutting down the channel out of fear or a sense of unworthiness impedes the flow. In that way, I am reminded to maintain the connection.

This evening as I was vacuuming my office, the door of which is labeled *Imaginarium,* I inadvertently shut off the surge protector into which the internet modem and the battery that charges the computer were plugged. I had no clue for some time as to why I didn't have internet access until I noticed once again that the computer was not operating at full capacity. Once I turned the strip back on, the internet and computer's energy were restored, as was my own.

So it seems that both the computer and I are Higher Powered. And with that, I cannot help but scream, bellow, yell, call out, and shout, "Charge!"

Bliss Kisses

In what ways do you sometimes 'disconnect' from your Source?

Do you believe that there is a never ending supply of love, money, inspiration, success—or do you believe that it is limited in some way?

Do you surround yourself with people who charge or drain your batteries?

How can you tap into the endless flow?

Chapter 13

A Relationship with Chocolate

*"There's nothing like a good friend.
Except a good friend with chocolate."*
—*Linda Grayson*

Chocolate is my 'drug of choice'—it always has been and likely always will be. Eaten in moderation, it is said to lower blood pressure, increase serotonin levels, and stimulate endorphins. Theobromine contributes to mood elevation, and phenylethylamine is said to bring on the same feelings we have when in love. Dark chocolate contains flavanoids, which are antioxidants that overcome the free radicals that age us. Now if all of those technical reasons aren't enough to send you to the candy store, how about the fact that chocolate makes your taste buds sing?

It is comfort food from childhood ... Hershey's Kisses®, M&M's®, Tastykakes®, Peppermint Patties®, and Girl Scout Thin Mint® cookies. Doesn't your mouth just water at the mere mention of the stuff? Vicarious experience not quite being the same as the real thing, you may want to have a morsel handy while reading the rest of this chapter.

Any book written by a woman on the subject of bliss would be incomplete, in my estimation, without covering chocolate (or perhaps being covered in chocolate—the woman, not the book). My friend Peter told me that most women he knows have a relationship with chocolate so strong that when they talk about it, it makes him blush. I can't help but wonder if it is hardwired into us and genetically pre-disposed; I think every woman I know on a personal level adores chocolate.

A chocolate massage, offered by my friends, was part of my birthday celebration when I turned 49. Sticky, but fun. Salons are now offering chocolate pedicures. It is an ingredient in skin care products, bubble baths, and perfumes.

A few years ago, I attended a yoga class taught by a delightful imp of a teacher from California named "Yeah Dave" Romanelli. The email announcing the class beckoned me with fingers curling seductively in my direction:

> *Join us for this creative and unique workshop taught by David 'Yeah Dave' Romanelli as he fuses the 5,000 year old practice of yoga with great modern music ranging from Frank Sinatra to Puff Daddy and everything in between to create Yeah Dave Yoga. The practice will be accented by tastings of chocolatier Katrina Markoff's Vosges Chocolate line to enjoy the sense of taste with a totally present state of mind. The ultimate sensory experience!*

The combination of chocolate, yoga, and music were irresistible. If the fourth element of sex had been offered, I imagined a packed house. I signed up immediately!

Yogaphoria, a delicious studio in New Hope, PA, was the site for a trip into heaven for this choco-holic/yoga-holic. I was intrigued by Dave's approach to the ancient art, bringing it from the esoteric to the contemporary. His youthful appearance and effervescent teaching style had this group of 20– to 50–somethings (mostly women—it's the chocolate connection) enjoying sweating to the various musical stylings that ran the gamut between Bob Marley, Bruce Springsteen, Aretha Franklin, Jerry Garcia, Peggy Lee, and India.Arie. Before the class, we were given a truffle that combined chocolate and chilies, followed by one that combined chocolate with curry and coconut. Dave's take is that chocolate—fully experienced—brings us to this moment. That is where the pleasure lives. And pleasure's address is the one I want to occupy as well.

During the class, Dave shared a quote by the author of *The Monk Who Sold His Ferrari*, Robin Sharma: "Life is a series of moments. You miss the moments, you miss your life." This is as easily applicable to eating chocolate as it is to anything else in life. Living in bliss is about savoring, relishing, and indulging in this moment as if it is the only one you will ever have. Given that knowledge, how would you choose to live it?

Biting into the first piece, I felt a burst of fire. Chili is not among my favorite taste sensations, but fused with the chocolate, it was mellowed enough to cause an *ahhh* to course through me. It was a perfect intro to the yoga practice, in which breathing is key. Anticipating the after practice treat (I know, anticipation pulled me out of the moment), I could feel my body stretching toward the morsel that was inches away. We were asked not to take the second piece until after completing the asanas. I allowed myself to gaze at it adoringly, still appreciating the piece I had enjoyed earlier. Maybe that is an element to a bliss-filled life as well . . . enjoying and appreciating what we are given in the moment AND looking toward the other goodies that await.

Bliss Kisses

In what ways do you allow yourself to live in the moment?

What pulls you out of present moment awareness?

How do you create fusions/blending of various aspects of your life?

Chapter 14

Thoughts That Do No Violence to My Soul

"Is it kind? Is it true? Is it necessary?"
—*Sathya Sai Baba*

On a crisp November night when the leaves carpeted Lancaster Avenue in Devon, Pennsylvania—creating a path to the door of YogaLife Institute—I gathered with other like-minded souls to engage in networking. As business cards and brochures were exchanged, it was a chance to be 'shamelessly self promoting'. I was able to meet some people for the first time and see others who represented the blast-from-the-past phenomenon that I love.

One was a man named Sean who, when I introduced myself to him, had a big grin on his face and reminded me that we had met in 1995 at an Omega Institute conference in NYC. The teacher and writer Robert Bly was at the conference, and I had wanted to interview him. Sean had guided me to Mr. Bly, and when I asked for an interview, he responded, "Why the heck would you want to interview me?" As this was 10 years ago, I wasn't able to think as quickly on my feet and was caught off guard. Today I would have volleyed back with something more eloquent that likely would have snagged the interview. Needless to say, I walked away without it. Sean and I had a good laugh about this night, a decade later.

A short while before leaving the event, I received an important message from the Universe. It was a poem from Jalal Al-Din Rumi, more commonly known as Rumi—the 13th century mystic Persian poet, whose works I think of as 'love poems to the Divine'. They are beautifully layered with meaning since they were written initially to praise his teacher, Shams-i-Tabrizi, as well as God. On the human level, many are delightfully conducive to romance.

The message I received this particular evening was on the bulletin board in the potty at YogaLife, and it spoke so profoundly to what I had been experiencing the prior few days. While it is incredibly tempting to shoo away the darker experiences and hold up our hands to shield our faces, I've learned that they are just as important as the tickled laughter of those happenings we welcome with open arms.

The Guest House

This being human is a guest house.
Every morning a new arrival.

A joy, a depression, a meanness, some momentary awareness comes as an unexpected visitor.

Welcome and entertain them all!
Even if they're a crowd of sorrows, who violently sweep your house empty of its furniture, still, treat each guest honorably.
He may be clearing you out for some new delight.

The dark thought, the shame, the malice, meet them at the door laughing, and invite them in.

Be grateful for whoever comes, because each has been sent as a guide from beyond.

On the way home, I was flipping through the radio stations and caught 'Delilah' on B-101, just after she played Steve Winwood's "Higher Love." She was speaking directly to me (and undoubtedly many others) when she asked if there was someone we were judging and wanting to control to do things our way. What if we could see them through that Higher Love? What transformations could take place? I'm muddling through that now as I have been going head-to-head with my 18-year-old son over some major life issues. Perhaps the answer is to go 'heart-to-heart' instead.

Violence is more than what comes from a clenched fist. It can come from a closed heart as well. One of my all time favorite wordsmiths is Richard Bach. I'm not sure what book this snippet came from, but he talks about having thoughts that do no violence to his soul. How often do we have self deprecating thoughts, or beliefs about others, that are toxic? I know that I do, fortunately on a less regular basis than I once did. I have also been questioning a concept that ties in with the knowing that we are God incarnate.

What if the God-that-I-am wants something different from the God-that-you-are? When I posed this query to various friends, unanimously they came up with the same answer: when we are in our God-selves, it doesn't matter who gets what outcome. It is when we are immersed in ego that shouts "I want it my way!" that pain and suffering ensue. There seems to be great importance in seeing 'other' as 'self'. This is the Rasta concept of 'I and I', rather than 'us and them'. I have been viewing my son Adam as being so dramatically different from me that at times that he will deliberately exaggerate the behavior to prove me right.

I am also learning the value of the three questions attributed to Indian spiritual teacher and guru Sathya Sai Baba: "Is it kind? Is it true? Is it necessary?" When I am mindful of these queries, I am far more likely to engage in 'right relations' and far less likely to enter into conflict. The 'kind and true' concepts are more easily integrated for me, while the 'necessary' is a challenge to my inner know-it-all. I ask myself why I feel a desire to share certain bits of information. Is it because I believe it will be truly helpful, or because it is self aggrandizing and ego stroking?

So, for this day at least, I vow to feed my soul with nourishment in the form of thoughts that serve the highest truth I know—that love is all we are, regardless of form or appearance.

Namaste.

Bliss Kisses

What thoughts do you hold that may be soul damaging?

Are you willing to release them?

Who has shown up at your Guest House?

Do you keep the door open or deadbolt it closed?

Chapter 15

Standing at the Crossroads

"What are four walls, anyway? They are what they contain. The house protects the dreamer. Unthinkably good things can happen, even late in the game. It's such a surprise."
—*Frances Mayes*

Tonight I watched one of my favorite movies: *Under The Tuscan Sun*. As always, I found myself immersed in emotion soup . . . laughter, tears, goosebumps and *aha* moments. Diane Lane plays a newly divorced writer named Frances Mayes who goes to Italy on vacation, sent there by her pregnant lesbian friend and her friend's partner. A series of cosmically coincidental meetings and celestial signs sprinkle throughout, and Frances buys a crumbling villa in Tuscany. She wistfully casts her desires for someone to cook for, a wedding to take place in the home, and a family to live there. Those wishes come to pass in profound and unexpected ways.

The most poignant part of the movie occurs when Frances is in conversation with Martini, the realtor she befriended who helped negotiate the purchase of the villa. She bemoans her circumstances, wondering if her life will ever turn around and allow her to feel a sense of home. He says to her:

> *Signora, between Austria and Italy, there is a section of the Alps called the Semmering. It is an impossibly steep, very high part of the mountains. They built a train track over these Alps to connect Vienna and Venice. They built these tracks even before there was a train in existence that could make the trip. They built it because they knew some day, the train would come.*

Someday the train will come. Each day I awaken and, like Frances, find myself 'standing at the crossroads', wondering which way to turn. I question why my life circumstances appear as they do at the moment and what steps to take to have them blossom more fully into what I desire. I gaze backward and see when and where I have laid the train tracks in impossibly steep mountainous terrain. I notice, with gratitude, who it is that has worked on the railroad with me, swinging the hammers and pounding steel into rocky ground. I question what it is that has me knowing eventually Vienna and Venice will connect and that the train will arrive, carrying on it the work I was born to do and the partner with whom to share my villa. Each day, like Frances, I celebrate the family of choice that embraces me and the beauty and magic that I encounter. Each day, like Frances, I notice the messages that arrive ushering me into "the four walls," in which, "unmistakably good things can happen, even late in the game."

Ciao, Bella.

Bliss Kisses

Do you feel as if you are standing at a crossroads in your life?

What wishes have you scattered out into the Universe?

In what ways have they come to pass?

Are you willing to get on the train and see where it takes you?

Chapter 16

Tattooed Angel

"Don't judge a book by its cover."
—common English phrase

Once upon a winter morning after digging out from under the second 'snowmaggedon' or 'snowpocalypse' of 2010, as it is fondly being referenced, I headed into work. Stopping at Dunkin' Donuts® for my treat of a cup of vanilla chai, I pulled into the snow-covered parking lot. Wishing I had a camera handy, I watched in amazement as an unlikely looking pair walked out of the store, arm-in-arm. A 20-something young man who was tall and tattooed with multiple body piercings including two in his lower lip, in addition to a 6" or so striped mohawk adorning his head, was escorting a petite, elderly, elegantly coiffed and garbed lady. He was helping her to her car so that she could safely traverse the erstwhile slippery sidewalk. She thanked him, and then I thanked him. I informed him that he had earned his wings this morning and that he had indeed made my day too. He seemed embarrassed by the praise and nodded in response.

Upon entering the store, I struck up a conversation with the woman in line in front of me. A woman in front of her turned around and gazed at me for a moment and then shook her finger in recognition saying, "I know you. What's your name?" When I told her, she grinned and said, "You married my husband and me." One of my many hats is that of an interfaith minister, and her wedding was among the first I officiated after my ordination in 1999. Now married ten years, they have a five-year-old son. I left the store smiling, the feeling buoying me as I drove the rest of the way to work.

I turned on the radio, listening to my local NPR station called WHYY and the show *Radio Times* with Marty Moss Coane. She was asking people to call in with snow stories and whatever cutesy titles they had for the snow storm. Powerless to resist, I called in and shared my morning experience. I called it 'cosmic snow-incidence' (a take-off on one of my favorite terms, 'cosmic coincidence'). Marty's delightful response was something to the tune of my being able to see past the tattoos and body piercings to the invisible wings he had sprouted. Perhaps they were there all along.

My friend Karen Drucker has a song called "We Are All Angels," in which she proclaims:

> *We are all angels, who only have one wing*
> *We are all angels, searching for each other.*
> *We are all angels, who can not reach the sky*
> *Because we need each other to fly.*

Imagine how much more joy we would experience if we knew that we were never without the angels in both celestial and human form. Each day I encounter them quite simply because I invite them in, notice them when they show up, and welcome them to stay.

Today I encountered angels at an event I attended sponsored by an organization called Enchanted Makeovers, which offers a variety of services, including rehabbing shelters and making them feel like home-away-from-home for folks without their own four walls. On this day, there were angels bearing handmade quilts with words like *compassion, faith, inspire, spirit,* and *strength* lovingly sewn into them; angels decorating and enjoying sweet treats; angels teaching and learning yoga and journal writing; an angel singing a song she wrote for this special day; angels applying makeup, styling hair and manicuring nails; angels painting a faerie-land mural; and angels painting gifts for their mommies who were attending the event.

The inspirational founding enchanting angel is Terry Grahl. In 2006, Terry was drawn to create her organization when someone she knew invited her to visit a homeless shelter. The drab, cold environment was not in and of itself inviting, but one item caught her attention on a metal bunk bed—a polka dotted pillow. Terry, a talented interior designer with a strong spiritual faith, felt called to offer her creative gifts. She has, in the interceding years, moved heaven and earth to create welcoming environments for those who pass through shelter doors.

I was asked to be the dinner speaker on the second night of the event held at York Street Project in Jersey City, New Jersey, called *The Journey... Discovering Our Inner Treasures*. It was my birthday weekend 2010, and I was the one who felt like I had received a tremendous gift by participating. Profoundly inspired by Terry, the other volunteers, and most especially the women who were the 'recipients' of the time and attention showered on them, I witnessed the heartening transformations and reminded them that they were no less beautiful before their 'makeovers'; the love had simply called their inner beauty forth.

May you recognize all the angelic beings in your life, including the one in the mirror.

Bliss Kisses

In what ways do you 'judge a book by its cover'?

Has your opinion changed once you got to know the person?

Have you witnessed random acts of kindness?

What angels are in your life?

How do you come to recognize them?

Are you willing to share your wings?

Chapter 17

The Cosmic Yes!

"We follow the path through the heart and into the Presence. When we get to the Presence through the heart ... yum, yum, yum!"
—Ram Dass

Last year, I spent the better part of a yummy weekend floating on the gently healing ripples of sound offered by a trio of musical devotees—Deva Premal, Miten, and Manose—as they descended on Philadelphia. I was enticed by the music from the very first note of the Gayatri Mantra, a sacred Hindu chant, that flowed from my radio five years ago on a show called *Echoes* on WXPN 88.5 FM in Philadelphia. The sweetly heart-penetrating voice of Deva carried me to such a state of transcendent bliss that I knew I wanted more. And there indeed was more to be had this particular weekend.

My friend Mahan Rishi Singh Khalsa, who is a dedicated Kundalini yoga teacher and chiropractor, hosted the concert last evening and chant workshop today. Six hundred or so singing souls took their seats in the Philadelphia Cathedral on Friday night, eagerly anticipating the treat that awaited them. Voices uplifted, we filled the sanctuary to the rafters with the names of the Divine, offered in a call-and-response manner known as kirtan.

Each is a talented musician in his or her own right, but together they create such an intricate weaving of beauty. As I shared with friends in a late night email after returning home from the concert:

> *The music was heaven sent and the silence after each chant allowed for reverberations of peace to wash over us. At most concerts, people are accustomed to applauding. At a kirtan, although it is entertaining, it is also sacred ritual, so clapping after each piece is*

discouraged. What magic these folks are . . . Deva is from Germany, raised by parents who were disciples of Rajneesh (also called Osho). Miten is from England, and his background is rock and blues. Manose is from Nepal, and his specialty is Indian bamboo flute. The feeling of the evening was, at turns, devotional, sensual, rowdy, still, meditative, playful, bluesy . . . altogether amazing. I laughed, cried, danced, prayed, meditated, chanted, sang, all in a 2 ½ hour period. I so love this kind of music . . . it is most certainly a way of feeling connection with all that IS.

Deva and Miten, as partners in music-making and life, have been together for 19 years and their 'home' is wherever they happen to be. Today, as Miten shared with a laugh at the workshop, it was Philadelphia. As they told me two years ago when I had the pleasure of interviewing them, the world is their home. Manose joined them on the road four years ago and his contribution to the trio is more than just support; it seems an essential component to their signature sound. He is indeed God's flautist, or perhaps the hollow reed itself.

The four hour workshop—not nearly long enough—held at the Elkins Estate in Elkins Park, PA, was a multi-modal experience in a much more intimate gathering. Eighty of us sat on a colorful sea of yoga mats, zafus (meditation cushions), and blankets as we took the chanting to a deeper level. In preparation, we completed breathing and movement exercises—tuning the instrument, as it were. For many of those present, chanting is part of our yogic practice and equally as sacred and supportive to our well-being as asanas (postures) on the mat. It feeds my soul and, in the case of this weekend, it healed my tired and cold-symptomatic body.

At one point we moved into a marble-floored grand entrance room that had a domed ceiling and sculpted figures, which appeared as if outstretched in ecstasy, embellishing the railings that hovered above us. We offered Sufi prayers, acknowledged the oneness of all life, and gave and received compassion. Performing Sufi circle dancing, we twirled and spun, held hands, gazed into each other's eyes, bowed and stretched in honoring the blessings in our lives, deeply grateful for it all. Love is the message in each syllable. The familiar chant 'om' is considered the sound of the Universe and, according to Deva, "The cosmic yes!"

One of my favorite chants is called "There Is So Much Magnificence," and we sang it together as we closed the day:

There is so much magnificence
Near the ocean
Waves are coming in
Waves are coming in
Hallelujah.

The men were asked to sing the first part of the lyrics, and the women were given the hallelujahs. What a divine delight to be serenaded by the Shivas (Divine masculine) in the room and for them to be showered in love by the Shaktis (Divine feminine) in the room. I cried during both parts, feeling overwhelmed with joy.

By the end of the workshop, we were all aglow; some 'strangers' in the beginning, now family, were brought together by a common desire to live the love that we are.

Bliss Kisses

How can you live in the 'yum zone'?

In what ways do you say a hardy cosmic yes?

Chapter 18

Beloved Bozos

"We're all bozos on the bus, so we might as well sit back and enjoy the ride."
—*Wavy Gravy*

One of the many perks of my job as a freelance journalist is being able to attend seminars and write about them for transformational publications. A few years ago, I was invited by The Omega Institute in Rhinebeck, NY to attend a weekend workshop and do just that. With excitement, I perused the catalog until I found the perfect weekend and the ideal workshop for me.

Called "Broken Open," it was based on the book by that name written by Elizabeth Lesser, one of the co-founders of Omega. Together with David Wilcox, one of my favorite singer-songwriters, and Nance Pettit, the amazing healing force and musician married to him, Elizabeth co-facilitated an experience that leaves me reeling and reveling as I continue to soak in the loving energy that followed me down from Rhinebeck. The description of the workshop didn't do it justice, but enticed me nonetheless. It spoke to my own seemingly broken places that called out for deep healing. This is the description that jumped off the page at me:

> *'And the time came when the risk to remain tight in a bud was more painful than the risk it took to blossom.'—Anaïs Nin*
>
> *Not just once, but over and over throughout our lives, each one of us is the bud whose time has come to break open. Usually, we fear change, loss, or transition. But these challenges—at work, home, in a relationship, or with our health—are the very experiences*

that can nudge us open and make us bolder, wiser, and more fully alive.

This experiential workshop is for anyone who wants to learn how to fight less with the changing nature of life and death, and relax more into the mystery of existence. We use meditation practice to put down the burden of the way it's supposed to be, and rest in the freedom of the way it is.

Through conversation, writing, listening to music, and engaging in healing and therapeutic exercises, we find the courage to dive into and through the difficulties of being human.

The participants came from all over the country, carrying with them their pain, wounds, secrets, and struggles as if they had packed them in their luggage. Courageously, the contents were unfolded in one another's presence, before open and receptive hearts. A group of 45 bonded rapidly when, on Friday night, we each briefly shared our stories.

Before I even entered the building, Elizabeth greeted me warmly, reminding me to keep the participants' identities confidential and asking me not to tell the group my purpose there initially. She felt it would detract from the totality of my own experience and encouraged me to be a full participant. Although I appreciated her guidance, I felt a clutch of fear and a sense of dishonesty. My monkey mind kicked in immediately and chattered in my ear: *What if people feel betrayed when they find out you've been undercover?*

I struggled with that even as I shared that what brought me to the workshop was a sense of needing to be real without hiding behind the various and sundry roles I play. My heart thudding throughout, I wondered if I was transparent and allowing people to see through my disguise. I did what I always do when the simian saboteur starts jumping about . . . I fed it a banana. Truth be told, I needed an entire backpack of them to keep her satisfied throughout the weekend. This time, the banana was a reminder to myself that I really did deserve the growth and learning at this paradise I had visited three times in as many summers. For those who haven't been to Omega, it is very much heaven on Earth, and I could feel the stressors of the week literally melting away when the car turned on to Centre Road. Let the sighing begin . . .

I found myself in the company of people who may have been feeling the same way that I did, but who dove in nevertheless. Music, meditation, experiential exercises and readings from Elizabeth's book highlighted the weekend. Although the workshop wasn't jam-packed with activity (unlike my life), it was rich in content and felt more like a gentle internal cleansing than a spiritual colonic. The co-mingled energies of Nance, David, and Elizabeth created a safe container for what transpired.

One of the chapters with which Elizabeth regaled us was "Bozos on the Bus." Many of you who lived during the 60's may recall Wavy Gravy, a clown who was the emcee at Woodstock. His contention is that we all have our frailties and vulnerabilities, we can all fall down and skin our knees, and we can all still come up smiling. He appears to be unafraid of looking silly and, in fact, relishes it. Elizabeth used the phrase "we are all bozos on the bus" throughout the workshop, encouraging us to allow the parts of ourselves that we are too cautious to unveil to come out in all their glory.

As I deepened my exploration, remnants from childhood decisions came clamoring for attention. One of the most powerful moments arrived during a heart opening exercise. Nance had asked us to be aware of our places of neediness. *Yikes!* I had lived so many of my 48 years attempting to deny that part of myself, replacing it with taking care of the needs of others. If these people in the workshop saw that I felt truly needy at times, what would they think? My place of neediness has been answered over and over by many people in my life . . . a desire to be known and seen, and a desire to be loved for who I am and not for what I do. No matter how many times and in how many ways the words were repeated, they still hadn't sunk into my being.

After we expressed our areas of vulnerability, our partner was to place their hand on our heart and send it "the perfect medicine to heal it." The words my partner offered me sent an arrow that pierced my heart and then provided the balm to heal it. She looked me straight in the eye and asked, "Do you think you're better than the rest of us? That we have needs and you don't?" What a wake up call. I honor her for that. For so long, I had been in that 'meeting needs' role because it felt frightening to ask for what *I* need.

The cerebral chimp chattered: *What if I don't get it?*

"Oh shut up. Here, have a banana."

So, here's a newsflash for y'all (and, maybe not) . . . sometimes, despite being surrounded by blessings and loving souls, I feel lonely, sad, scared, angry, doubting, judgmental, and jealous. My ego-mind can throw a whopper of a temper tantrum. A few months ago, someone challenged me to be aware of the places in my life where I had suffered and may still be suffering. I told him that I knew from his Buddhist perspective what he meant by suffering, but I still resisted even considering the possibility.

As the layers of facade were stripped away, I felt closer to these folks—they were part of my new family of choice, and during off workshop time I found myself engaged in conversation, the likes of which I would normally have held (even as open as I am) with people I've known at least a little longer. We faced each other in all of our perfect imperfection, holding each other literally and figuratively through it. A wave of emotion enveloped me: ecstatic joy mixed with profound grief.

The cumulative energy of so many people simultaneously on their individual healing journey can be overwhelming for me at times. On the last day, I awoke at 4:42 a.m. with a message in the form of a question: "How much of yourself are you willing to bring to the table?" That morning, Elizabeth asked if people had anything to share that had arisen since last night. I raised my hand and 'came clean' with the group about my dual role as journalist and participant. No one was shocked. I assured them of their confidentiality and Elizabeth reinforced that. As I wept for all the times I had been inauthentic in my life, assuming the role of a caregiver when I wanted to be a care receiver, people whose issues seemed far more acute than mine at the moment reached out to embrace me. In doing so, I think it strengthened them as well.

The last exercise we did to close out the workshop had us symbolically placing into a pine cone what 'it' was we wanted to release and then throwing it into a fire, declaring what we wanted to rise like a phoenix from the ashes. I asked to surrender the belief that I can't be vulnerable or needy and still receive love, and then I did something that is uncharacteristic for me—I said that I had no clue what would arise. For the first time in ages, I really didn't have answers, but instead stated that I was gonna have a great time watching to see what emerged.

So, from this Bozo to all my Beloved Bozos who are reading this . . . climb on-board the bus, and let your tears and laughter blend, so you don't know where one begins—and where the other ends.

Bliss Kisses

In what ways do you fear appearing foolish?

How do you hold back fun, love, playfulness?

Would it be so much more fulfilling to risk 'looking like a bozo'?

Chapter 19

Validation

"I only attract loving people in my world for they are a mirror of what I am."
—Louise Hay

The Universe speaks to me (and to us all, if we listen) through friends. Last night, my friend Peggy Tileston was the conduit through which deep wisdom arose. She sent me an email that linked me to a beautiful 15 minute video that you can view by going to a website called *Daily Good* http://www.dailygood.org/more.php?n=3583.

The action takes place through the metaphor of a customer service counter and then spreads exponentially in a 'pay it forward' manner. Initially, the tongue in cheek meaning of the word 'validation' was pretty mundane, and then the powerful message came through that we all thrive on validation—not just for what is seen on the outside, but also on the beauty that shines from within. How often do we offer that to ourselves or each other? As we age, the mirror can become a place that we dread visiting, because in it we see lines, wrinkles, and the toll that the years may have taken on us. Imagine instead that the mirror is a metaphor for the ways in which the world views us and reflects back whatever it is that we are putting forth.

I invite you to take a few moments right now to be your own cheerleader. Come up with a least five inner qualities or aspects of yourself and at least five outer qualities that you can can validate. You can even do this in a mirror and—if you are feeling really brave—a full length mirror . . . naked. Last year I met with a woman who said she had her first spiritual experience at age three when she gazed in the mirror and asked, "Who's in there?" So, I encourage you to ask yourself the same question. You may be surprised at what answers come through.

The response may be different each time you inquire. You can make it a daily practice.

Once you have done this, the next step is to offer that sense of unconditional loving kindness to your family, co-workers, and even people you meet as you go about your day. Imagine the impact.

Bliss Kisses

How do you validate yourself?

How do you invalidate yourself?

When you feel good about yourself, how does it impact your relationships?

How does your world reflect back that which you are?

When was the last time you courageously gazed into the eyes of the person in the mirror?

Chapter 20

Living Orgasmically

"Electric flesh-arrows... traversing the body. A rainbow of color strikes the eyelids. A foam of music falls over the ears. It is the gong of the orgasm."
—*Anaïs Nin*

What would it be like to live your life full out, allowing the rich juiciness of who you truly are ... to ooze, to ripple, to burst forth in all its glory? I feel exhilarated just typing that question. Heart racing, blood pumping, vivid imagination soaring off into all kinds of dazzling places. Take a breath ...

Are you in that delicious place in your life, living in technicolor? Or do your days feel like a series of one mundane experience following another? My desire is for you to dwell in the first land, but if you are simply existing in the second, I extend my hand and invite you to cross the line that divides one from the other.

How to do that, you ponder?

The first step is to recognize that you were born with senses that drink in the wonders of the world around you. What you don't use, you lose; our sensory apparatus, like any other tool, gets dull or rusty if we let it sit around for too long. When was the last time you entered into a day seeing, smelling, tasting, touching, and hearing what surrounded you? Tomorrow morning, when you awaken, do a check-in ... what is the first thing you notice with each of your senses? You may even want to journal what you observe. Make it a daily practice.

The next step is to be aware that you deserve pleasure. Long ago I gave up the idea of 'guilty pleasure', knowing that what I experience guilt-free benefits me far more and serves as an example to others. Recently I heard the song "What's So Bad (About Feeling Good)?"

by singer-songwriter Ben Lee, and the chorus shares, "No guilt. All pleasure." Love it! It's my new theme song.

It's also important to recognize that we experience pleasure from three perspectives. The first is in anticipation. Think about something on your horizon that really excites you. Feel that adrenalin, those butterflies in the stomach, that *YES!* resonating through you. Imagine the experience as if it is occurring in this very moment. Breathe into it. Then move to the second perspective, which is the experience itself. Be totally present in it, keeping those lovely senses alive to it all. For example, if in the presence of a lover, refrain from thinking about the laundry, the bills to be paid, and the lawn that needs mowing while that person's body is enwrapped and enraptured with yours. Lastly, we experience pleasure in memory. All it takes to evoke the feelings is to mindfully recall them; like magic, our bodies' innumerable talented receptors and cells help us facilitate the experience of pleasure over and over again.

Attune your body to the key of 'O' as you live an orgasmic life. Orgasm is far more than a physiological response to sexual stimulation. Experiment with walking through your day in that state. What turns you on? It could be dancing, wearing clothing that floats over your body, allowing massaging hands to caress your skin, watching the sun dapple through newly green leaves on a gorgeous early spring day, smelling the aroma of fresh baked chocolate chip cookies wafting from the kitchen followed by the sweetness of the chocolate melting on your tongue, or listening to the voice of a beloved whispering in your ear. Those are some of my favorite delights from my ever-expanding list. I am sighing as I call them in.

When my now 24-year-old son was a child and given the choice between two different flavors of ice cream, he would reply, "I want both of each." What a concept—both of each. He wasn't willing to be limited and neither should you. So, what's your pleasure? And how have you been putting a dam in your own pleasure-stream? Imagine the possibilities . . .

I have come to learn that the imagination is the most powerful aphrodisiac. One of the benefits of being a writer is that I am able to immortalize my experiences afterward, being certain to keep the confidentiality of anyone else involved, of course. Whether you are a writer or not, I offer the following suggestions to you:

1. When sexually stimulated orgasm does occur, whether in the company of someone else or solo, allow yourself to breathe into the experience. By doing so, you increase the energy and the pleasure, extending the ripples in the proverbial pond outward farther and longer.

2. Be fully expressed by telling those in your life what you like. First, know what you like by becoming familiar with your body and its delicious responses to pleasure. Experiment with ways in which you enjoy touching and being touched.

3. Sometimes it's a matter of quieting the voice that harangues, "Good girls and boys don't . . ." I have found that when the chattering monkey mind plagues me with limiting thoughts, it's best to distract it by feeding it a chocolate dipped frozen banana. Monkeys like love and attention too!

Also, surround yourself with 'pleasure ho's'. Many of the people in my inner circle would proudly pin that label on themselves. They slurp all of the juice from the bottom of the glass, sing and dance way past full, feel frequently fascinated, go for the gold . . . and they inspire me to do the same. I believe that like attracts like, so by identifying yourself in that way, you will absolutely draw those kindred spirits into your world.

The late philosopher, author, and speaker, Joseph Campbell coined the phrase, "Follow your bliss." I believe in taking it a step further and teaching people to BE their bliss, since by simply 'following', we are still seeking someone or something else to fulfill us. I have learned that I am the source of my own pleasure, and from that state I invite others in to play along with me. Come join the dance and transform the ordinary into the extraordinary!

Bliss Kisses

When you think of the word 'orgasm', what comes to mind?

Who do you believe is responsible for your pleasure?

Are you concerned about what 'the propriety police' will think about your quest for the highest bliss?

Are you willing to release the belief in 'guilty pleasures', and instead simply allow for them?

I invite you to make a list of what lights you up from the inside and turns you into a human sparkler. List your top 10 pleasures:

Chapter 21

Poetic License

"The real voyage of discovery consists not in seeking new landscapes, but in having new eyes."
—*Marcel Proust*

While driving along the highway of life, signs and messages appear to guide us. They are course corrections that lead us back to the main roads when we are tempted to take unnecessary detours. The same is true for the infrastructure on which our cars travel. I love reading license plates and gleaning meaning from them, and I offer here some pretty cool examples of ways in which they have spoken to me over the years. Some are humorous, others poignant.

The first that comes to mind showed up a few years back. I was on my way to perform a wedding ceremony at a lovely little chapel in New Hope, which is an artsy town nestled along the Delaware River in Pennsylvania. Imagine Haight-Ashbury and Greenwich Village—it is perhaps a bit more family oriented, but you get the picture.

Having taken a wrong turn, I was running uncharacteristically late and attempted to reach the couple via cell phone. No luck. Out loud, I sent a message on the 'cosmic telegraph', telling them (and myself) that I would be there soon. A moment later, back on the correct road, a car pulled in front of me and I laughed when I saw the letter configuration **NVR2LTE**! Can you figure that one out? It assured me that I am always at the right place at the right time. I arrived with moments to spare, officiated the wedding, and had a delightful story to share. In case you didn't get it . . . *Never Too Late*.

Three years earlier, I was driving on Rte 309 outside of Philadelphia, and I received a call from my mother in Florida. She shared that the time had come to make a dreaded yet necessarily anticipated trip southward as my father, Moish, was about to make his transition. For three years,

Parkinson's Disease had its way with this formerly vigorous, vibrant man, who had six pack abs into his seventies and who worked in a gym well into his eighties.

On autopilot, I turned back toward home to pack and purchase an emergency plane ticket. I was feeling quite numb; the tears were working their way to the forefront and then burst forth as I beheld another traveling billboard of spiritual significance. This time the license plate said **LVMYDTR**. This one, I read as *Love My Daughter*. As I am writing these pages tonight, I am honoring the second anniversary of his passing—this man who called me "doll baby," taught me to ride a bike, fly a kite, roller skate, box (thank goodness I became a pacifist, since I could have developed a mean right hook), and shared paternal wisdom that serves me to this day.

I call them 'Moishisms': "They put their pants on one leg at a time, just like you do." "Your life is in the hands of any fool who makes you lose your temper." "If that's the worst thing that ever happens to you, you'll be ok." And, in the midst of a few adolescent head butting sessions, "As long as we love each other . . ."

Last weekend, I took a much more pleasant trip a few hours south to the nation's capital and was feeling rather fatigued—the result of excessive amounts of work sprinkled with nowhere near enough play and veg time. As I was about to nod off, a license plate message jolted me awake as it proclaimed **NRG4U**. Ok, Universe, I get it. *Energy For You*. I gratefully received the recharge. A short while later, I was pondering the twists and turns my life has taken and feeling appreciative of the beyond amazing people who have been companions on the journey. As if on cue, a car moved ahead of me, leaving in its wake the message **GR8FULL**. *Grateful*, of course.

Like many people I know, I have had the welcome mat out to bring into my life a soulmate/partner. Widowed more than 11 years ago, I have since been blessed with wonderful friends and lovers, knowing that love is never wasted. For this trip, I had brought a book on the subject of attracting the One and curled up on a comfy chair in the suburban Washington, DC home of friends Michael and Patti. I drank in the information and began practicing the exercises. The next day, while homeward bound, I lit up when I saw yet a third harbinger. This time, the Divine had seen fit to place before me this luscious combo: **SOLEM8** . . . *Soulmate*.

I wish you mystical messages and joy along your journey as well.

Bliss Kisses

Where is your personal journey taking you?

What signs do you pay attention to?

What has been the outcome?

What signs have you ignored?

What have been the consequences?

Chapter 22

Dance Like Everyone Is Watching

"Dance like no one is watching. Sing like no one is listening. Love like you've never been hurt, and live like it's heaven on Earth."
—*Mark Twain*

On a frigid Philly night I brought my friend Jaz, who had lately come cross-country from warmer California climes, to a must-see location glorified in the musical query, "Where do all the hippies meet?" Ten extra bliss points if you can answer it before you read the name.

South Street is an artsy, vibrantly colorful bastion of outrageous activity at nearly all hours. Bars, restaurants, and eclectic stores hawk wares ranging from books that will help you raise your kundalini, to 'adult toys' that will raise something a little less esoteric. One such dining establishment is called Johnny Rockets, which beckoned us into its radiant warmth and had us rolling back in time to the 1950's. The décor, menu, and uniforms of the wait staff all screamed *Happy Days*. I half expected Richie Cunningham and 'The Fonz' to come peeking around the corner.

We slid into the cushioned booth and ordered hot chocolate embellished with gobs of whipped cream to melt away the chill in our bones before immersing ourselves in sandwiches and onion rings. He and I spoke about our life passions, as we often do. Jaz is a dreamer extraordinaire and he mirrors my own creative soul, all the while encouraging me to live life full out. Everyone should have at least one person in their life like him. As we were deep in conversation, the lights dimmed and the 1978 Donna Summer hit "Last Dance" came bounding out of the stereo. The staff lined up in front of the booths and began steppin' out to the music. I watched in wonder as they swayed in time, engaging the customers in their antics. Jaz cajoled me to join them. Uncharacteristically, I sat back, feeling suddenly shy. "Next song," I promised him and myself. I asked our waitress, an adorable 20-something, when that would be.

"Oh, in about 30 minutes or so," she responded.

"If we are still here then, I'll join you," I said, half hoping that we would finish and scoot on out before I embarrassed myself.

It was not to be, as 30 minutes zipped past and the Brothers Gibb began their ascent with the "wings of heaven on their shoes" and the cross between groaning and sighing chorus of "ah, ah, ah, ah stayin' alive, stayin' alive" bouncing off the candy apple red booths.

"Now's your chance," Jaz grinned broadly. Being a woman of my word, I bopped up and took my place next to the other dancers, most of whom were young enough to be my children. I asked our waitress, who was standing beside me, to count off the steps so I could follow along. Within moments, I was in the groove. Twirling, spinning, and hand jiving, I was actually keeping up; what a freeing feeling. I looked back and caught my friend watching me with feeling of pride and an 'atta girl' smile shining through his beard.

When the music ended and the customers clapped their approval, I experienced such a rush of exhilaration—a true on-top-of-the-world emotion. We walked out of the 1950's and back into the year 2009, and somehow the wind seemed to have ceased blowing. The cold wasn't quite as penetrating either since I was warmed from the inside by dancing my joy (and burning off calories in the process). All in all, not a bad way to spend part of a Friday night.

Bliss Kisses

In what ways do you 'dance like everyone is watching'?

When was the last time you took a step outside of your comfort zone and did something that seems uncharacteristic for you?

Who encourages you to do that?

What would it take?

Are you willing to do that today?

Chapter 23

Mammogram Mambo

"Save the ta-tas®"
—*www.savethetatas.com*

Tonight I returned from a necessary part of self care that most women find, at the very least, unpleasant; many find it downright torturous. It began with the donning of a designer cotton gown and ended with my needing to fluff up two of my favorite body parts, assuring them that I still loved them and—as a result—paradoxically exposed them to compression that had them screeching for mercy.

I told Deanna, the wonderful tech who in her career has likely treated thousands of women to this form of TLC, that there should be a sticker given out after the mammogram like those given out after donating blood. It could say, "Be nice to me, I just had sensitive body parts flattened like pierogies," or "I just did the hokey pokey with a machine: you put your right breast in, you take your right breast out." I have seen all kinds of humorous messages blazoned across t-shirts and bumper stickers from "Save the ta-tas" to "Throw out breast cancer, save second base" as a means of encouraging women to have mammograms.

In the spring of 2009, I reconnected with a dear friend from Willingboro High School from whence I graduated in 1977; he and I hadn't spoken for 30 years. Along with Abe came the gift of his wife, Andi Morris . . . a definite Goddess Sister and kindred spirit. A Center City Philadelphia area realtor, Andi is also a two time breast cancer survivor who shares, "I was diagnosed when I was 37, and then, when I was 43, I was re-diagnosed." With the initial diagnosis, she was frightened and shocked. With the second diagnosis came anger, "because I was working so hard to get beyond breast cancer."

Andi has a full, rich life that includes travel, returning to work, and volunteering for an amazing organization called Living Beyond

Breast Cancer. An active board member and dynamic public speaker, Andi testified in front of the FDA in favor of silicone implants for breast cancer survivors. She recognizes how fortunate she is to have had phenomenal treatment and solid support systems. This delightful woman with a contagious laugh seems to have a 'there but for the grace' attitude and expresses, "It has been my passion and pleasure to give back in any way I can."

I came face-to-face with this thriver (by my definition, someone who has surpassed survivor mode and reaches out to help others because of his or her own experience), who has made such a difference in the lives of so many through her fundraising and educational endeavors, when I joined a group of 200 some brave souls gathered on the steps of the Philadelphia Museum of Art on May 17, 2009. This same structure made famous by the pounding feet and upraised arms of Rocky was the holy ground for a gentler endeavor—the *7th Annual Yoga Unites For Living Beyond Breast Cancer*. More than $100,000 was raised on a day which carried wind gusts that threatened to blow us into the Schuylkill River.

When I arrived, the gray over-hanging clouds loomed ominously, and the steps were already puddled and slippery. Finding a space to lay down my purple 'magic carpet' as I sometimes call it, my mat snuggled in between others already in place. As I stood from the next-to-top tier of the steps and gazed downward, I beheld with delight a rainbow sea of mats and people gathered—all ages, all body sizes, all levels of yoga-expertise, some familiar faces from the yoga community (which I have come to know has some of the biggest hearts in the world), and some new companions in the mission to support survivors in re-creating their lives. We were becoming family of choice and chance.

The team of friends that surrounded her during the yoga event is coyly called "Andi's Girls," which is a double entendre in reference to her reconstructed breasts that she refers to as "the girls." She adds, "It keeps me laughing."

To help ensure that others keep laughing in the midst of their own challenges while they live with and beyond breast cancer, please visit www.lbbc.org.

Bliss Kisses—*these questions are a bit more serious:*

What are your thoughts about your breasts?

Do you view them as parts of your body to be hidden?

Were you taught that they are for the pleasure of a partner or only for feeding babies?

Do you know how to do personal breast exam?

How often do you do so?

When was the last time you had a professional exam to help maintain breast health?

Chapter 24

Mala

"When you inhale, you are taking the strength from God. When you exhale, it represents the service you are giving to the world."
—B.K.S. Iyengar

This was quite an auspicious weekend, bringing with it energy that flows through me and out from my fingertips onto the keyboard. The fall equinox, Yom Kippur, the United Nations International Day of Peace, and a series of events called Global Mala Project all coalesced over the past 72 hours.

The Global Mala project www.globalmala.com is the brain/heartchild of yoga teacher Shiva Rea who put out the call to people of conscience and action to make a difference not only this weekend, but every day. Most who practice yoga set an intention for that time, and the mat becomes a place of personal fulfillment as well as a platform of sorts to send out loving energy to all life. When practiced with others or, as Shiva Rea expressed it on the website, "Yoga Lokah" (the global yoga community), it is that much more powerful. It was from that thought that this movement was born. All over the planet, yoga studios planned events to connect the world. Is it a pipe dream that yogis and yoginis, sweating on their mats from LA to PA, from India to Israel, from Brazil to Bali, from Pakistan to Peru, could effect change on a planetary level? I don't think so. And likely neither do the thousands of others (maybe millions?) who participated, including those who may still be engaged in their events as I am typing this at 8:30 p.m. EST on Sunday evening.

Rewinding the clock, before I weave the story around my own experience . . .

For many years, since my late teens, my time on Yom Kippur was spent in nature, communing with the Divine. This year, I ventured up river (the Delaware) to Stockton, NJ where I sat by a tide pool that fed the larger body of water as it tumbled through the locks and over stone worn away by thousands of years of rushing liquid. Moments before clambering down the side of a hill and claiming a space on a flat rock, I stood transfixed for a brief time, leaning over a wooden bridge, gazing at the pond below. At first I wasn't sure of the origin of the ripples and whether they came from lightly falling raindrops or the miniature fish that swam beneath the surface. As I continued to watch, it became clear that the aqua-life was creating the movement.

Ring after ring of water intersected and danced into and through each other; it was the perfect metaphor for what I was to experience this entire weekend. As I sat on the rock and meditated, I felt called to pick up small pebbles sunk into the dark sandy soil. I asked for them to be part of my ritual. The High Holy Days are about *'t'shuvah'* or *'turning'*, as in turning over a new leaf (perfect for autumnal change), or turning away from what no longer serves and turning toward what most nourishes us and all life. One by one, I imbued the stones with my fears, limitations, hesitations, and self deprecation, and I cast them into the waiting water. Satisfying ker-plunks met my ears each time. Then I chose other stones and into them placed my intentions for this new year. Acceptance of love and abundance in all forms, being of greater service, stepping forward instead of retreating while simultaneously taking time to go within and simply be, being compassionate and gentle with myself—these were my focus.

I had brought with me a *japa mala* (in Sanskrit, the word *'mala'* means *'necklace'*), which is a beautiful symbolic tool to keep one's mind focused on meditation and prayer. 108 is considered an auspicious number in the cultures that use them. There are 109 beads on the mala. The 109th bead is called the sumeru, bindu, stupa, Buddha, or guru bead. Counting should always begin with a bead next to it. In Tibetan Buddhism, one mala constitutes 100 recitations of a mantra. There are 8 additional recitations done to ensure proper concentration. In yogic tradition, it is explained that originally there were 54 sounds in the Sanskrit alphabet. 54 x 2 = 108. There are 108 Upanishads, the sacred Vedic texts. 108 is also the result of multiplying 9 and 12, two propitious numbers in Indian culture.

As I gathered about me my own devotional practice, the names of people who are important in my life and those who I love came to mind. Family, friends, teachers, guides, mentors, lovers—those living and those who have passed on—all fair game. Their names became my mantra; their faces became my prayer. Twice around the mala, 216 people. I sent out love and blessings for their Highest Good. I could have gone on longer, calling to mind the names of all of those who have been important to me throughout my life, but I would still be sitting there. I marveled at how blessed I am to have at least 216 people to name in my heart and mind. One name reminded me of another, perhaps the person who had introduced me to the next one in line, who introduced me to the next, and so on. By the time I left, I was floating to my next destination.

Which returns me to the Global Mala group experience. I headed to Stillpoint Yoga, the studio of my friends Jack and Debra in King of Prussia, PA. There we were called on to offer up 54 sun salutations. Also called Surya Namaskar, this series of postures honors and greets the sun. This was followed by 54 minutes of trance dance. These, together, added up to the number 108. Since the Global Mala Project is for the purpose of raising money as well as awareness, the charity of choice was The Hunger Project.

As around 20 of us stood poised on our mats, beloved yoga teacher Yoganand Michael Carroll, who had been offering a teacher training, led us in an invocation that all beings know peace, love, and healing. Debra then began the process, dividing the asanas into manageable cycles of 18. The first was to send love and blessings to ourselves, the second to our immediate community, and the third to the world. She counted off each one with an individual mala bead that she transferred from one bowl to another. No longer feeling like my mat was a magic carpet as I have come to think of it at times, but rather a surf board on an ocean of breath (also, less spiritually, because it was becoming wringing wet with sweat), I felt like I was transcending the ache and the mind chatter that would have had me quit from fatigue before it was over.

By the time we reached the end of the third round, I felt so euphoric that I could have gone on longer. In conversation with others who stayed and enjoyed the dancing and pot luck veggie dinner, I found that they felt the same. That's the beauty and power of practicing in community. A fellow yoga student decided to forgo the physical practice, instead gracing us with his chanting and guitar playing as support for our endeavor. Live music always helps.

As this weekend comes to a close, I am aware of feeling inextricably linked to each soul. One by one, we are the beads of the mala—stringing, connecting to the next and the next, beyond 108 and out into infinity. Namaste.

Bliss Kisses

When you count your blessings, how many can you contemplate?

Think about the people in your life who bless you and whom you bless.

Through your thoughts and actions (in a sense, taking your 'yoga off the mat'), how can you become a greater force for good in the world?

Chapter 25

Godwinks

"That's too coincidental to be a coincidence."
—*Yogi Berra*

I am aware of phenomenon that occur daily, which I refer to as 'cosmic coincidence'. These are all of the synchronicities that, without paying attention, happen all the time anyway. They include everything from the phone ringing with a friend whose face or name just crossed my consciousness on the other end to finding the perfect parking spot. In our family, we refer to them as 'Uncle Jimmy spots', since my mother's brother Jim always found the ideal parking spot no matter where he went. I received a book as a gift recently called *When God Winks On Love*, and it describes the multitude of romantic relationships that began with what the author SQuire (yes, that's how he spells it, with the capital 'S' and capital 'Q') Rushnell refers to as a 'Godwink', which is a means of getting the cosmic ok on the steps we take.

Recently I experienced several of them, back to back. After work one Thursday night, I stopped at a craft store for a drawing pad my son Adam had requested. He was particular about the one he wanted, so on my way in I affirmed, "I always find what I need." I found the right pad and walked out. Then I added a little zip to it and said, "I always attract everything I want and need in my life for my Highest Good, and I always attract my heart's desire." I figured, what the heck?

I was on my way to a meeting for Rubye's Kids, an organization that sponsors an annual holiday party for over 400 inner city kids in Philadelphia, PA. I had time for dinner and was driving along Route 611, leaving it open to the Universe as to where I would stop. Energy started buzzing when I came to this diner called Bonnet Lane. I'd driven past it before but had never stopped. The car practically turned itself into the lot. I walked in and, wonder of wonders, it was St. Patrick's

Day in October—complete with Irish music and menu. What made this so poignant was that my friend Greg had just returned from a trip to the Emerald Isle, and the day before he had regaled me with stories of miracles that transpired while he was there. When I told him about the experience, he jokingly (I think) indicated that knowing I was coming, they set it up just for me to see. Shades of *Twilight Zone* or *Outer Limits*.

I brought Julia Cameron's book, *The Artist's Way*, which is a course of study for artists, writers, performers, and all kinds of creative types. A waitress approached me and asked what I was reading. Then she proceeded to tell me out of the clear blue that she was writing a book with the concept of 'what if?' and how certain decisions we make lead to events that we never would have imagined.

She also told me about her work in helping other parents whose children are addicts. I told her that I work at an acute care psychiatric hospital, and she related her time in college when she completed a practicum there herself. I opened the book and the subject discussed on the page before me was synchronicity! Before I left, I stopped in the potty and saw a woman at the sink washing her hands with her back to me. When she turned around, I realized it was my friend Kathleen Pleasants, whom I hadn't seen in close to a year. You could have knocked me over with a feather at the amazing chain of events. Although I am used to this, I still shake my head in bewilderment at times.

Tonight I was at a gathering at my friend Maria Starr's house, and I struck up a conversation with a man with whom I sensed I needed to speak. It turns out that we had more in common than I thought, from similar early religious indoctrination that now has us heading in a different direction, to the healing of our hearts. We also had several friends in common as well as books and teachers who inspire us. What qualifies this as an interesting Godwink is that in 1987, when each of us got married, we had outdoor weddings officiated by the same minister!

I invite you to keep your eyes and hearts open to the multitude of Godwinks that occur, not only daily, but oodles of times each day. Please don't let them pass by without being acknowledged. I tend to think that miracles like to be noticed too.

Bliss Kisses

What Godwinks have occurred in your life?

Do you dismiss them as inconsequential?

What belief would you have to release to accept them as valid?

Chapter 26

Zen Starbucks

"Everyone has a spirit that can be refined, a body that can be trained in some manner, a suitable path to follow. You are here to realize your inner divinity and manifest your innate enlightenment."
—Morihei Ueshiba

You can find enlightenment at any time and in any place. One night it zapped me in the Starbucks™ at the corner of State and Main in Doylestown, PA. There I sprawled in a comfy chair across a low table from my friend Deev Murphy (short for Diva, as she told someone to whom I introduced her) as we sipped favorite drinks—coffee for her, chai for me. Deev is a work of art herself . . . colorful, inspiration, and imagination incarnate.

Her new project is gathering creative souls together to help her paint a "1989 dark gray Buick Sky Hawk into an art car, covered with suns & stars & swirls of galaxies, and on both sides, the words *dream, believe, achieve,* and *inspire*." Imagine the conversation that branched out from there. We were talking about relationships, and she shared a bit of well-meaning, but rather flawed (in my humble opinion) wisdom that came from her mother who told her that your partner is responsible for 90% of your happiness and unhappiness. I countered with the thought that if you allow someone else to be your source of happiness or unhappiness, you are always at the mercy of someone else's whims and actions.

Then she asked me what I felt I could count on for certain in my life. I said, "only two things—that I was born and that someday I will die." Every person in our lives is on loan to us and every experience passes. Change is the only inevitability, and that can be frightening or exhilarating. These days, I'm leaning toward exhilaration.

From there, we meandered into one of the most challenging spiritual lessons I encounter, and perhaps the same is true for you. She referred to the concept of emptying out . . . totally letting go of it all to allow for the new and healthy to enter our lives. The beautifully simple example she gave was of changing the water in her cat's dish. She doesn't just top off the water—she empties the used water out. She doesn't just add new water—she washes the dish. Even then, she takes it a step further by wiping it dry to remove any remaining residue. And from that point, she doesn't just add tap water. For her cat's well-being, she replaces it with distilled water. This entire process may only take a few minutes, but it is powerfully symbolic of the care that we can also put into our own clearing process.

In order to fully let go, I know I need to trust implicitly that I can live with the in-between, not knowing, in the meantime, free-fall stage. Terrifying at times, it embodies my spiritual amnesia, because inevitably the answer, the re-fill, the manna-festation (as my friend Kim Walker calls it) arrives even more gloriously than I could have imagined. I forget at times that all is well and in Divine order. I am there now in my life, as daily I let go of all I thought I knew to be true.

Surrendering over and over my old beliefs, expectations, understandings, and perceptions of the people in my life . . . just letting be. I would call it a cosmic colonic: a complete and total psycho-spiritual cleanse. Sometimes the cleanse comes in the form of tears that accompany a painful revelation, as happened on my drive to meet Deev after work that evening. Sometimes it arrives as a side-splitting laugh at work in recognition of an inside joke shared with a coworker. Mostly it is there through the process of life, in the ebbs and flows of relationships and interactions—being willing to give it all up to allow for something even better. Let's make a Divine deal. Door number one or curtain number two? It's anybody's guess. Either way, you win.

Bliss Kisses

When you think about emptying out, what comes to mind?

In order to make room for what you want, you need to create space. What needs to move on so that you can attract something even better?

What fear holds you back?

Chapter 27

Fantabulous 50!

*"I have enjoyed greatly the second blooming...
suddenly you find—at the age of 50, say—that
a whole new life has opened before you."*
—*Agatha Christie*

I turned 50 on October 13, 2008. The birthday cards are still taped to a door in my hallway so that I can see them as soon as I walk in the house. They are reminders of how loved I feel for when I become spiritually amnesiac. I intend to keep them up there at least until I turn 51.

My generous friend Lisa Balter hosted my party and gathered together kindred spirits from all along the corridor that runs from Pennsylvania and New Jersey to Virginia. Luscious food, laughter, affection, sweet gifts, and a rather raunchy poem conspiratorially constructed by lasciviously creative folks who had nothing better to do on their three plus hour ride northward to the party, were all part of the festivities.

After dinner, we gathered in a circle and I was offered tribute as I sat on the floor, legs outstretched before me, feeling all of 5 going on 50. Or was it 50 going on 5? Friend after friend shared their thoughts about our connection as I remained there, so wanting to drink it, but instead I felt like the Teflon shields were up and all the loving words simply slid off like a sunny side up egg on a frying pan. I wish that I had thought to audio or videotape the experience to replay when desired. Like anything in our lives, the cellular memory lingers and my heart remembers.

Entering into the next half century felt like crossing over a threshold that I had culturally been taught meant that I was going to dry up in all ways. That couldn't, as I have discovered, been further from the truth. In many ways I feel fuller, richer, and juicier than ever. I take emotional risks that I never would have a decade ago. I tumble willingly into joy-filled times. As I am writing this book, I am dared by friends and by life itself to truly live my bliss. In honor of my 50 years on the planet, I have listed 50 experiences and items I choose to call into my life to celebrate my incarnation on the planet this time around. I have experienced some of these and want others. I'll leave it up to your imagination to guess which is which.

1. Daily massage
2. Monthly pedicure
3. Vacation in Hawaii
4. Standing under a water fall and swimming in a tide pool in Hawaii
5. Traveling to the UK
6. Kissing the Blarney Stone
7. A personal trainer to work with me and get this body in healthier condition
8. A vegetarian cook
9. Dancing
10. Drumming
11. Retreats to Omega, Kripalu, and Esalen—teaching there as well
12. Multi-handed massage
13. Sunset in Mallory Square, Key West with a nonalcoholic "Last Mango in Paradise"
14. Skinny dipping

15. Daily yoga classes in a studio

16. Soaking in a hot tub daily

17. A makeover

18. Writing for whatever magazines I would like

19. Meeting SARK

20. Meeting and marrying my Beloved

21. Living in a beautiful home in the woods near a lake

22. Writing best selling books, starting with this one

23. Speaking at conferences, expos, and on book tours

24. Enjoying breakfast in bed

25. Being breakfast in bed

26. A chocolate bubble bath in a deep tub

27. Photography classes

28. Ballroom dance lessons

29. Getting a beautiful sari

30. Being on Oprah's show

31. Being on Ellen's show

32. Facilitating a Cuddle Party at the White House

33. Having a soft-top Jeep® again

34. Letting my nails grow long enough to have a regular manicure

35. Getting a henna tattoo

36. Redoing my wardrobe

37. Renovating my kitchen

38. Renovating my bathroom

39. Having plenty of money to use, save, and share

40. Traveling to Sedona

41. Visiting the Grand Canyon

42. Taking voice lessons

43. Creating CD's and DVD's

44. Daily gym 'play-outs' (way more fun than calling them 'workouts')

45. Interviewing Oprah

46. Shedding 50 pounds and keeping it off

47. Teaching classes worldwide

48. Traveling to India

49. Taking art classes

50. Return to swimming regularly

Bliss Kisses

So, what's on your 'loving you' list?

Do you dare to live into these visions for yourself?

What could possibly hold you back?

Chapter 28

Blowing Bubbles with Mom

"Walk in like you own the joint."
—Selma Weinstein

Spring 2010 had me zipping up and down the East Coast on metallic airplane wings that often felt like wings of angels as I dove headfirst into an experience that many of you have already had or may be involved with at the moment. My Dad passed in April of 2008, and my Mom's health had been seesawing back and forth since then. Earlier in the year, her primary care doc—a dedicated, funny, compassionate man named Dr. Montes—told us that due to congestive heart failure, kidney disease, and diabetes, my Mom might not be with us much longer. As has been the case in our family, she was determined to make each 24 hour period precious and meaningful, and we clearly told him that she would be his miracle patient and far outlast his prognosis. Not panicking or catastrophizing, she was still expressive of lingering fears, but with her days mostly infused with joy.

My sister Jan and I made the trek to Ft. Lauderdale to spend time with her. The first round had her more actively engaged; we went out to get her hair cut into an adorable elfin look that was easier to take care of and style. Yet within a few days of returning home, we were both summoned by her doctor since she was in crisis mode.

My mind whirled with all of the anticipatory tasks. I wear many hats, and among them include medical social worker and minister. I am also my mother's power of attorney and executor of her will. All of those roles stood in protective mode in front of the daughter who wondered if she would return from this trip an orphan. I packed as if I would be performing her funeral, planning her eulogy in my head en route.

When I arrived at the hospital, I beheld the woman who had raised me with love and empowerment looking frail and pale. Machines made their necessary noises as they monitored her vital signs and pumped oxygen. The trickling waterfall sound of the humidifier reminded us of a flowing stream on which we traveled to parts unknown. She remained on that unit for a few days and, on one particular day, Dr. Montes delivered the news that she was going to be transferred to the hospice unit of a sister hospital. A deep gulp and a sense of inevitability washed over me.

I was, however, comforted by the knowledge that she and we would receive excellent care. The hospital called Memorial Pembroke offers hospice care through VITAS and is staffed by angels in scrubs. From the nurses and doctors to the chaplain, and from the social worker to housekeeping staff and volunteers, we were immersed in a peace-filled and nurturing environment.

Sleep came rarely and fitfully as I camped out on a couch in the Quiet Room next to my Mom's, or in her room on the love seat with my legs hanging over the edge. At times I sat in the chair next to her bed, holding her hand, watching her every breath. Our conversation during the wee hours often turned to what she thought would happen when she died. More questions than answers, it seemed. I reminded her when she does pass to tell me what's out there. We sang a lot—songs from my childhood and hers, as well as those from musicals. I discovered that she enjoyed opera, and she wistfully shared that at one time she had "an almost operatic singing voice."

While I was with her, I had the mixed blessing of being able to write copiously, including this book. The computer became an emotional life line as it kept me in touch with friends who offered loving support throughout. One missive sent to them:

> *My immediate world at the moment is this room and my Mom, tending to her needs while the rest of my 'normal' life is seemingly 'out there'. . . . my usual routine feels so far away even as I continue to write and the words pour forth in ways they didn't before. Emotional roller coaster. I had a thought last night, that she was 'wisping away' and it brought tears. And then . . . her doc feels she may be stable enough to go home early next week which I am thrilled about. I brought her Miracle Bubbles (we'll take a miracle any way it shows up) and we have been playing with them; part fun, part respiratory therapy. She laughed with delight. No need*

for pain meds today, nor breathing treatment since yesterday in the wee hours.

Wonder where she goes in her thoughts when she sleeps.

Bizarre cosmic coincidence as we watched the movie 'Beetlejuice' tonight and I told her that I didn't think the afterlife looked like that . . . good thing, huh?

One of things we decided was that she was going to leave the hospice unit 'vertical', and a week later she was one of two who did just that. Many others there, in God's Waiting Room, passed from this realm into whatever greeted them upon their arrival.

At this writing, my Mom is home receiving care from hospice and her caregiver Claudia, who makes her laugh and brings along the mop-top side-kick therapy dog wanna-be named Disney, an adorable Yorkie. She plays with my Mom and sits protectively by her side or on her lap. We speak three times a day now and sometimes her response when I ask her how she is doing is, "Hangin' in there, baby." And at others, "Soon."

Early on she had been ambulatory with a walker, sitting on her porch when able, and going out back to look at her banana tree in early summer. She still has visits from friends and watches her shows, but she now sleeps more than she is awake. She reminds me at times: "I still have my marbles, or at least most of them." I told her that I could retrieve those that may have rolled under the couch. And then there are moments when she feels they are wandering from her grasp.

Her dreams are vivid and seem to be progressively preparing her for what might await. Having been a bereavement counselor for many years, I have learned that 'travel talk' and dreams that contain other loved ones who have passed are an invitation to progress toward death. A few months ago, when I asked her if she thought my father would be waiting for her, she told me "I don't know." A few weeks ago, she replied in response to my question, "I hope so." And on what would have been their 54th anniversary on October 14th, she clearly stated, "Yes. He told me he would come for me."

Ironically not too long before that, she had a dream in which they were walking on a beach together. When he had died, she kept his wedding ring. In the dream, she put the ring back on his finger, and he thanked her for returning it to him. A short while later after awakening, she noticed that the ring had disappeared from the nightstand where she had kept it. Everyone searched high and low, and it was nowhere to be found. Maybe sleeping dream-state and waking dream-state are one in the same . . .

I count my blessings each time she answers the phone, and yet I know there will come a morning that I will not need that instrument to communicate with her, instead just a tuning in with my heart.

Bliss Kisses

What relationships do you value, knowing that each day is precious?

How do you face your own mortality and that of people you love?

Chapter 29

S'Mores in Heaven

"The mark of your ignorance is the depth of your belief in injustice and tragedy. What the caterpillar calls the end of the world, the Master calls the butterfly."
—*Richard Bach*

I began writing this final chapter sitting comfortably in a blue and gray tweed seat onboard the Amtrak Auto Train en route from Sanford, Florida to Lorton, Virginia. I gazed out the window waiting for the train to take me to my new life—one without parents physically accompanying me. My father took his leave on April 3, 2008, and my mother joined him on November 26, 2010. She passed peacefully, with the hospice nurse by her side.

Orchestrating it perfectly, my mother made sure that neither my sister, nor I, nor her devoted live-in caregiver Claudia were present. I had spoken with her earlier in the week, asking if she wanted me to spend Thanksgiving with her and she declined, telling me it wasn't necessary and that she was ok. I reminded her that it was likely, then, that I wouldn't be there until the very end. I fully anticipated holding her hand and watching her take her final breath. It wasn't to be.

By Wednesday, when I called her for our morning check in, she told me she didn't want to talk. When I contacted her on Thanksgiving, to tell her I love her, her voice was barely audible. The next morning, I spoke with the hospice nurse, who informed me that this formerly vigorous woman "was very weak" and couldn't speak. I asked the nurse to kiss her for me. I then heard the voice in my head say clearly, "Mom is never going to call you again," and the tears began to flow. A few minutes later, I said to my father: "Take care of her now," and then corrected it. "Take care of each other."

Less than an hour later, my sister called and informed me that our mother had just died. My reaction was visceral, as a howl of *"Oh no!"* emerged and the sobbing began. As I sat at my desk at my full-time job as a social worker in a psychiatric hospital, it occurred to me that now there was no rush to travel the 1200 miles south to the home in which she and my Dad moved in 1989. She was already gone. When my father died, I arrived four hours prior to the time his heart stopped counting out the flow of his life.

My sister and I traveled from our respective homes of New Jersey and Pennsylvania, girding ourselves for the ordeal of being motherless daughters. As I entered the Philadelphia International Airport, a smile lit my face. "She did it again," I thought, choosing likely the least busy travel day, since it was the day after Thanksgiving and most people were still likely at their destinations.

My mother's Toyota Camry® is tucked in with the other autos, hopefully playing nicely. It is filled with well packed boxes that represent more than 20 years of the life that she and my father shared in Ft. Lauderdale—and the three decades prior to that. It amazes me when I consider how objects are both personal and impersonal. In reality, they are not flesh and blood beings, but they reflect the style, sense, and sensibility of their owner. Elegant and playful clothing to be donated to The Salvation Army®, which I know she would like other women to enjoy, are waiting in bags in her front hallway. Kitchenware in one of the boxes that I remember from my childhood include a glass rolling pin, a hard-boiled egg slicer, and (I will endeavor to describe it here) a wide plastic straw-like object with serrated edges that is to be dug into an orange so that the juice can be sucked out. A tarnished silver teapot brought over as one of the few possessions of my Russian immigrant paternal grandmother is nestled amidst the newspaper wrapped 'good china' that we used at Passover.

My thoughts spin back to a phone conversation a few weeks ago when her mind was still sharp and her 'gravel Gertie voice' as I referred to it, since her constricted breathing made it hard to project, was still comprehensible. Often we would take imaginary trips together—sometimes going ice skating on a pond, bundled in warm clothing, sipping hot chocolate afterward. Other times we would go to a park and play on the swings, our feet feeling like they were touching the sky, or ride on beautifully painted white alabaster horses on a carousel. Her favorite place to 'visit' was Hawaii, since although she and my father traveled extensively in their later years, they had never visited the 50th state.

"So Mom," I inquired, "Where are we going today?"

With little girl excitement, she responded, "Oh, we're going to Hawaii, to a luau. But no roast pig."

"Ok. A kosher luau, then. And what will we do there?"

"We'll dance the hula and get lei-d."

I grinned, knowing that she meant having leis draped over our heads. "So, two wild women out on the town, getting lei-d. I like that idea."

She joined me in raucous laughter. And then I asked what we would be eating at the festive occasion.

"S'mores."

For the uninitiated, s'mores are a yummy and decadent combo of graham crackers, melted marshmallows, and chocolate bars. My mother and I share a love of most things sweet—chocolate being a lifelong drug of choice. "Mom, I don't think they serve s'mores at luaus. I would bet that they serve s'mores in Heaven."

"I hope so," was her delighted answer.

I will have to wait until she tells me if that is the case.

In one of our earlier conversations, she told me that she would come back as a butterfly. Since her passing, countless butterflies and other 'Mom Miracles' have shown up—so many that their stories could fill another book. I will share a few here.

The day of my Mom's death, my cousin Jody Rosenblum ferried me to the airport. On the way, there was a car in front of us with a butterfly sticker on the rear windshield. Today, I was taking care of banking business and was setting up a page where I could monitor the account online. The young man who was setting it up showed me an icon that had popped up on the page, and guess what it was? A butterfly, of course. I laughed and explained why. He said that there were thousands of icons to choose from, and that was the first one that came up . . .

My Mom's neighbor Dianne came to pick us up at the airport and shared a story: she had agreed to give the funeral home the outfit my Mom had wanted to wear—it was the lovely and elegant suit she wore for their 50th anniversary vow renewal that I had the joy of officiating four years ago, and it was hanging on the back of the door of the den. Well, Dianne had forgotten to give it to them and went about tidying up with another neighbor, Myrna. Myrna remarked to Dianne . . . "That door to the den just closed by itself," and she was too freaked out to go in, so Dianne did.

Dianne laughed when she saw that the outfit was still on the door and said, "That was just Selma reminding me about the suit." She then got it over to the funeral home.

As my sister and I were pulling up to the chapel, we saw a butterfly dancing over the building. Prior to the service, we were greeted by one of my Mom's hospice nurses named Juanita, who loves pins. My Mom had given her a few of them, and the one she wore today was decorated with the winged wonders. I officiated the service remarkably calmly (enough for the funeral director to ask me afterward if I could come down there and perform them for other families), and we drove to the graveside escorted by a host of butterflies which, according to the funeral director, are rare there this time of year. As I was offering prayers before they lowered my mother's coffin into the waiting earth, another hovered above. Even as I am immersed in grief, I am heartened by the certainty that she is soaring freely and that my heart is as well.

Sitting in Starbucks, my 'office' while on the road, I heard two songs with serendipitous lyrics. The first was the hymn, "I'll Fly Away":

> *Some bright morning when this life is o'er*
> *I'll fly away*
> *To that home on God's celestial shore*
> *I'll fly away.*

The second song was by Shelby Lynne called "Gotta Get Back," with the rollicking chorus:

> *Gotta get back do I do . . .*
> *Butterflies take control me*
> *Why's this airplane go so slowly*
> *Flutter faster take me home to you*

On my return flight, I encountered an angel in human body in the form of a flight attendant named Jewelee (yes that is really her name, and she really is a jewel) who saw that I had SARK's newest book on my lap, *Glad No Matter What*, which is about healing, loss, and grief. I had just interviewed SARK and brought the book along for comfort. Jewelee exclaimed, "Oh, I love her!" and then walked past.

I went back to the galley with the book and loaned it to her while we were flying. I told her why I had it with me, and her tears welled up. She explained that a dear friend of hers had died and that she had gotten a tattoo in her friend's honor. When I asked what it was, she hiked up her skirt to show me a dragonfly on her thigh. Not quite a butterfly—but close. We hugged and cried together, and then a little while later she checked on me. We spent the next 30 minutes or so talking, and no one complained. We have remained in contact since then and delight in hearing about each others' lives.

I am now living my new life as an 'adult orphan' but feeling a sense of calm that comes from a certainty that they are both well. I am also relieved that I won't be waiting for the phone to ring with the news. Now there are no more parents to bury.

It is springtime. The crocuses are peeking their heads from the recently frozen earth and my self-protective-so-I-could-function heart is thawing as well. Last week was my Mom's 87th Birthday and tomorrow is the 3rd anniversary of my Dad's death, so I am in emotion soup, savoring the experience as best I can, which is an odd way to describe grief. But in its own strange way, it can be as nourishing as joy. I am ab-soul-utely certain that my parents are with me as I wind down this chapter in my life. My Mom had told me a few months before she passed that she wanted to read the finished book. I laughed, saying that she needed to live a whole lot longer, and I read her a few of the chapters instead. With a mother's pride, she said I had to complete the book. And so I have.

Bliss Kisses

What are your beliefs about an afterlife?

Have you received messages from loved ones who have passed?

Can you allow yourself to laugh in the midst of grief, having a full human experience?

Chapter 30

Bliss Bites

These delicious little nibbles are fat, calorie, and cholesterol free treats in which you can indulge at your leisure.

Dance Your Dreams To Life
Wiggle your toes at first and then, as the music in your heart grows louder and more insistent, sway back and forth. Feel the melody rise up your body until you move about the room with wild abandon or stand in sweet stillness. That too is the dance.

Play The Music Of Your Soul
Close your eyes and breathe in your soul notes. They are as unique as you are. Exhale harmony as they blend with those of the beings with whom you share this planet. Your song is worthy of a Grammy.

Make Magic Happen Every Moment
You are truly an alchemist who can turn lead into gold. Find a magic word and make it your own. At the mention of this mantra, your world is transformed. Frowns turn upside down, broken hearts are mended, and im-possible dreams become I'm-possible realities.

Let Your Love Flow
Imagine yourself to be a clear, running stream. Then allow yourself to overflow your banks, nourishing the flowers and grass that lace the edge. In every encounter you have with another, the healing energy of love spills over as they scoop up the precious handfuls and carry it to the next person they meet. Who could ever thirst?

Tickle Your Fancy

Discover ways to make the edges of your mouth curl up. This could be by taking a walk in the woods or savoring a decadent treat. You know that fat, calories, and cholesterol don't count if you indulge with joy. There is no such thing as 'guilty pleasure'.

Color With Your Creative Juices

When you were born, you were given an entire box of brand new crayons and an unlimited imagination with which to paint a rainbow design on the landscape of your future. Remember to color outside the lines.

Wander Whimsically

The next chance you get, go somewhere you have never been before, without benefit of map or compass. Turn right, turn left, guided only by your intuition. You will be astounded when you arrive.

Practice (Com)passion

When you are enthusiastic about something or someone, know that you are 'God-infused', which is the definition of the word. You are One with all that IS. When there is no 'other', how can there be an enemy?

Feel Frequently Fascinated

Boredom is a state of mind. Take a look around you. An entire universe was created for your delight. Kneel down in the grass and witness what is going on in that microscopic realm. Gaze up at the stars and drink in the splendor. Wonder what will occur in the next moment. Say hmmmm . . . a lot.

Learn About Love

Love is not a commodity to be traded in exchange for security, comfort, or companionship. The source of love is not another person. It is within you and emanates from the One Source. Love heals. Love with abandon and without fear of being abandoned. No one will ever love you enough to make up for you not loving yourself.

Greet Your God(dess) Self In The Mirror

Know that you and everyone else is a spark of the Divine that can never be diminished by life circumstance. What if you could honor that each day? What grand act of love and creation would come out of that question? The Sanskrit word *Namaste* means "The Divine in me recognizes the Divine in You." You are Divinely Human and Humanly Divine.

Shift Your Perception
The best definition of a miracle that I know is a shift in perception. Each moment, we have the opportunity to view the world through the crystal clear eyes of love or the distorted lens of fear. Be open to the messages that come your way, whispering, cajoling, singing, and shouting for your attention. Be miracle minded. Live a joy drenched life!

Be A Generous Giver And Gracious Receiver
We are taught that it is better to give than to receive. How can there be a giver if there is no receiver? Allow for the flow of both in your life. This is an abundant place in which we live and the Universe is waiting to offer you the gifts that are tagged with your name. When you are feeling rich (emotionally, spiritually, and materially), it is so easy to overflow into the lives of others. You can't give whatcha' don't got. You are worthy to receive!

AdoRe-sources

This is a list of people, places and products that I adore. They offer inspiration and information. I invite you to meander, visit their web pages, contact them, and support their work—as their work supports the world.

Agape International www.agapelive.com A community in Los Angeles that embodies the concept of unconditional love, combining New Thought/Ancient Wisdom. Dr. Michael Bernard Beckwith is the minister/spiritual leader, and Rickie Byars Beckwith is the director of the Agape Choir.

Angelwood Productions www.claimyourpower.net Candy Danzis is known as The Main Stream Mystic and an eager teacher of intuitive arts and angelic wisdom. She is an inspirational speaker who walks her talk. She is the creator of the Claim Your Power Conference.

Anusara Yoga www.anusara.com Founded by John Friend in 1997, Anusara yoga is a school of hatha yoga, which unifies a life-affirming Shiva-Shakti Tantric philosophy of intrinsic goodness with Universal Principles of Alignment. It is the mode of yoga that gets my shakti flowing.

Sera Beak www.serabeak.com Sera is the author of *The Red Book: A Deliciously Unorthodox Approach to Igniting Your Divine Spark*, the forthcoming book *Redvolution: Dare to Disturb the Universe*, and director of the upcoming feature film also entitled *Redvolution*. She is most certainly a Bliss Mistress who lives a vibrantly red-olicius life, red-olent with juicy flavor.

Kimberly Krause Berg www.Cre8pc.com Webmaster for Live In Joy. Kim is a website usability/SEO consultant, industry writer, speaker, and columnist on search engine marketing and usability. Kim is my web angel.

Christine Baeza www.elementalessence.net Christine is a visionary and a creative force whose technical aptitude and business savvy have positioned her as an expert in her field. By applying her international fashion design experience, life coaching skills, and her own spiritual journey to her entrepreneurial prowess, Christine instills hope and inspiration in everything she does.

Beliefnet www.beliefnet.com A place to explore what it means to be humanly divine and divinely human that includes articles written by transformational speakers and authors. It also offers inspiring videos and a place to offer and request prayers. Check out my Bliss Blog! http://blog.beliefnet.com/blissblog/

Joan Borysenko www.joanborysenko.com An inspiring writer and speaker, Joan is a pioneer in integrative medicine. She simply and succinctly communicates the interconnection between the body, mind, and spirit. She is the author of many books, including *Fried: Why You Burn Out and How To Revive* and *Inner Peace For Busy Women*.

Irene Bojczuk www.returntocenter.com I describe Irene as a lovingly kick-ass coach who guided me in preparation to complete this book, including helping me move on in my life by inviting me to drop my hyphenated last name as a way of changing the energy. She incorporates the Sedona Method, The Work of Byron Katie, and Rebirthing in her work with clients.

Albert Borris www.albertborris.com Albert is an extraordinarily insightful writer whom I have had the joy of knowing since college days. His book entitled *Crash into Me* is a wonderful guide for parents and professionals who love and/or work with teens. For kids, it offers a listening ear as they may come away with a sense of 'this guy really gets us'. Even for adults who are contemplating suicide, it offers insights and wisdom.

Creative Communication Builders
www.creativecommunicationbuilders.com
Janet Berkowitz and Phil Garber are the intrepid teachers and performers who offer colorfully creative classes and presentations for adults and children on physical and mental health issues, substance abuse prevention, bullying prevention, and team building.

Center For Conscious Living www.newthoughtccl.org An interfaith community in the heart of South Jersey, the Center For Conscious Living is a welcoming place to explore spirituality of the heart. Their motto is "Change Your Thinking, Change Your Life."

Center For Spiritual Living www.cslphilly.com A welcoming spiritual community that inspires personal transformation and positive change in the world, the Center For Spiritual Living is another New Thought church that promotes celebration of life.

Deb Chamberlin www.debchamberlin.com I refer to Deb as a 'Rockin' Mama', since she IS a mother, we met at a concert she organized for a group called Go-Girls, and she is also involved with Mamapalooza (tag-line 'Moms Rock!'). She is a peace and social justice activist and singer-songwriter, whose two major claims to fame are that she ran away with the circus in her 20's and is a jingle singer who was the voice of the Pennsylvania Lottery theme song.

Circle of Miracles www.circleofmiracles.org This non-denominational community in beautiful Bucks County, PA asks these important questions: "Who am I? Why am I here? What do I want?" Much of its focus is inspired by *A Course in Miracles* and Reiki.

Alan Cohen www.alancohen.com Alan has been a dear friend for more than 30 years. He is a motivational speaker, author, and radio talk show host. His show on Hay House Radio is called *Get Real With Alan Cohen.*

Common Ground Fellowship www.commongroundfellowship.com A non-denominational gathering outside of Philadelphia, Common Ground makes the definitive statement: "Whatever the question, love is the answer." Its monthly services feature the amazing Common Ground Choir whose music I describe as 'interfaith gospel'.

Cuddle Party www.cuddleparty.com A workshop that focuses on communication, boundary setting, safe and nurturing, non-sexual touch for adults. I bless the founders, Reid Mihalko and Marcia Baczynski, each day for creating this growing worldwide phenom, since I am a delighted certified facilitator.

Dawn of a New Day www.dawnofanewday.com Designed by Dawn Light, this site profiles and highlights people, ideas, and products for life enhancement and delight. She is also the author of *Dawn of A New Day Raw Desserts*. I have savored the decadently luscious raw chocolate she has prepared.

Diva Toolbox www.divatoolbox.com Diva Toolbox is a literary gathering place in cyberspace on which articles that help bring out your inner diva are available for your reading pleasure. I am a contributor to this site.

Divine Caroline www.divinecaroline.com Divine Caroline is a site that invites women to experience more pleasure while it informs and enlightens. It is another place that welcomes my writing.

Jim Donovan www.jimdonovan.com The friend who reminded me that this book wasn't doing anyone any good in my head, Jim is a powerful life coach, author, and transformational speaker. He tells you in every way that you CAN live the life of your dreams.

Lew Doty www.lewdoty.com A musical master at play in the Universe, Lew's songs inspire dreaming all that is possible. A spiritual marvel!

Veronica Drake www.veronicadrake.net Veronica's mission is to "empower women all around the world." She is a messenger for Spirit and is remarkably on target with the wisdom she shares.

Karen Drucker www.karendrucker.com Karen is a human sparkler-spiritual-singer-songwriter whose music accompanies me on the road.

She and I are aligned in kicking out our rather well developed inner critics.

Susan Duval Seminars www.susanduvalseminars.com Susan is a networker and promoter extraordinaire. The joke in our community is that whoever I don't know, Susan knows and vice versa. She brings in top-notch speakers, psychics, intuitives, and healers.

DV8Fitness www.dv8fitness.com Phil Scarito is a fitness trainer who works with the whole person to assist with form and function, flexibility, strength, and conditioning.

Enchanted Makeovers www.enchantedmakeovers.org is the labor of love of Terry Grahl and many volunteers whose creativity and passion transform shelters and the lives of those who go into them.

Arielle Ford www.arielleford.com Arielle is an author, publicist, and marketing wiz who puts heart into the art of promotion. She is also a firm believer in calling in one's soulmate using the Law of Attraction . . . proof positive, since she met her husband Brian with those tools.

Michael Franti www.michaelfranti.com The front man for the life affirming hip hop, rap reggae group called Spearhead, Michael is a practicing yogi and peace activist.

Gift of Life Donor Program www.donors1.org Serving the Delaware Valley (Philadelphia area), this organization provides education on the vital issue of organ and tissue donation. It is also the most successful organ procurement organization in the country.

Gilda's Club www.gildasclub.org Founded after the passing of versatile comedian and *Saturday Night Live* alum Gilda Radner, it offers solace, support, and empowerment to those living with cancer and their families. I have enjoyed volunteering for them.

Glitterati Art www.glitteratiart.com Handmade, one of a kind, dazzling keepsakes, including cards, clothing, and wall hangings. The artiste is my Goddess friend Dianne Evans.

Cynthia Greb www.cynthiagreb.com is a visionary artist, teacher, photographer, and interfaith minister who loves this beautiful planet. She holds the vision of a transformed and harmonious Earth. Her passions include working to bring more balance and joy into her own life and inspiring others to fulfill their dreams. Through both of these things, she is helping to create a more peaceful world.

Holistic Fitness by Mike Thomas www.holisticfitnessbymikethomas.com is a creation of this NSCA Personal Trainer who incorporates the best of East and West in his work with clients. One simple question he asked, launched me on a substantial weight loss journey.

Inspire Me Today www.inspiremetoday.com Created by the generous and kind-hearted Gail Lynne Goodwin, this site brings into the world the words of people she refers to as 'luminaries'. I am honored to be among them.

In Your Prime www.inyourprimeonline.com *In Your Prime* is a monthly magazine for those in the 55+ demographic. I joke that they let me write for them even though they began publishing my column called "Living Juicy" when I was still in my 40's.

Dr. Yvonne Kaye www.yvonnekaye.com Yvonne is a dynamic presenter on the subjects of humor, healing, grief, and women's empowerment. She is also an interfaith minister. Yvonne has been my mentor for over 20 years.

Jody Kessler www.jodykessler.com Jody is a passionate singer-songwriter and musician whose lyrics and music emerge from deep within, have taught me about 'leaps of faith' and when they come forth, audiences are delighted.

Kids Music Experience www.kidsmusicexperience.com The Kids Music Experience is a national service of music and song enrichment for kids at preschools and daycare centers. Peter Moses and his team of talented performers/educators bring the joy of music to young people's lives.

Kathy Davis Designs www.Kathydavis.com Greeting cards, posters, calendars, stationary, t-shirts, and other gifts with a rainbow-hued creative flair. For more than five years, I was a freelance text writer and one of those I refer to as the 'elves'.

Kinetics Magazine www.kineticsmagazine.com Published by Dannion and Kathryn Brinkley, *Kinetics Magazine* is a monthly publication featuring articles on spirituality and healing.

The Laughter Yoga Institute www.laughteryoga.org My friends Jeffrey Briar and Peggy Tileston are certified laughter yoga instructors. Laughter yoga was developed by Dr. Madan Kataria in India and has spread worldwide through laughter clubs.

Peter Makena www.petermakena.com is the transcendent musician who penned the song "There Is So Much Magnificence Near the Ocean" and believes that "The voice is an expression of the spirit, and like the eyes and the face, the voice is a window to the soul!"

Pamela Maliniak www.pampens.com is the editor extraordinaire who helped to birth *Bliss Mistress*. She is a creative communicator with a unique take on the written word. She has a gift for seeing the potential in each paragraph, polishing it like a precious pearl.

Mamapalooza www.mamapalooza.com Founded by Joy Rose of the all women rock band Housewives on Prozac, this festival honors mothers and proudly proclaims, "Moms Rock!"

Manose www.manosemusic.com I was introduced to Manose's music via his traveling partnership with Deva Premal and Miten. He is a modern day Krishna on bamboo flute.

MauiVision www.mauivision.net A gem on the tropical island that reaches the mainland. As they publish my articles, I have said that my writing has gotten there first, planting the seeds for me to travel there.

Molly Sunshine www.mollysunshinetour.com Molly Nece is the tour de force behind The Molly Sushine Tour that empowers people to live their dreams. This dynamo brings people together and encourages them to shine brightly.

Moving Creations www.movingcreationsinc.org Emily Nussdorfer is the dancing diva and mentor for this program that offers inner city young women a chance to shine through performance art. I call them her 'dancing Goddesses'.

Mt. Eden Retreat www.mountedenretreat.com Each time I travel the tree-lined driveway of this 'heaven on Earth', I feel like I am Home. This oasis in central New Jersey is the home of the delightful Jewish Mother Goddess, Delane Lipka.

Music for People www.musicforpeople.org Founded by Grammy award-winning Maverick cellist, David Darling, this organization invites people to make their own kind of music regardless of what they were told about their ability to sing or play an instrument.

Music in the Moment www.musicinthemoment.com Ron Kravitz brings his love for all things musical to individuals and groups in the form of workshops, retreats, and classes, as well as a weekly drumming circles that I get to whenever I can. He is a graduate of Music For People.

Dr. Murray Needleman www.murrayneedleman.com Murray has been a staple in my life for more than 20 years since his voice graced the airwaves in Philadelphia. He is a therapist of the most powerful type, and in a conversation many years ago he asked me, "Can you love yourself 'as is'?" That poignant question set me on a journey of internal exploration.

David Newman and Mira www.davidnewmanmusic.com Beautiful bhaktis, David and Mira are world traveling kirtan (Sanskrit chant) artists who hail from the Philadelphia area.

Off the Mat and Into the World™ www.offthematandintotheworld.org Created by renowned yoga teachers and activists Seane Corn, Hala Khouri, and Suzanne Sterling, they developed the Seva Challenge, encouraging people to stretch into spiritual and social activism.

Omega Institute www.eomega.org An oasis nestled in the Hudson Valley and located in Rhinebeck, NY since 1977, this holistic retreat center boasts the best in speakers and teachers. I sigh every time I go there for a weekend retreat.

Patricia Omoqui www.patriciaomoqui.com Patricia is a sister wordsmith, poet, life coach, and speaker whose subject matter is gleaned from the beauty of life, her two angelic children, and amazing husband.

One World Many Hearts www.oneworldmanyhearts.com Dedicated yogini and teacher, Brittany Policastro has raised money to travel to distant places and offer seva (service). She is affiliated with Off the Mat and Into The World.

Dr. Judith Orloff www.judithorloff.com Judith blends mainstream psychiatry with the power of intuition. She is a speaker and author of the bestsellers *Emotional Freedom* and *Second Sight*.

Pebble Hill Church www.pebblehillchurch.org Located in Doylestown, PA, this interfaith community has beautiful indoor and outdoor space for ceremonies and casual receptions. It is first and foremost a peace site and gathering place for people who wish to celebrate their spirituality with kindred spirits.

P'Nai Or www.pnaior-phila.org With innovative approaches to Judaism, P'Nai Or was founded by Rabbi Zalman Schacter-Shalomi and celebrates diversity.

Deva Premal and Miten www.devapremalmiten.com This musical power couple have long been a staple in my auric collection, starting at the moment I first heard Deva sing the Gayatri Mantra.

Stephen Redding www.stephenredding.com Stephen, author of *Something More* and *More or Less*, has died multiple times and "lived to tell about it." In these books, he shares stories of being run over by a tractor at age four, frozen to a fence in a blizzard at age eight, ultimately surviving multiple motor vehicle accidents and—most recently—surviving the stings of swarming yellow jackets. He is also an advocate for nature and preserving our precious resources. Like Dr. Seuss' *The Lorax*, he "speaks for the trees."

Robin Renee www.robinrenee.com The shakti-drenched songbird of Mantra-Pop blends a variety of musical styles in her sultry performances.

Felicia Rose www.feliciarose.com Felicia is a divine diva whose music tickles the soul and touches the heart.

Rubye's Kids www.rubyeskids.org Since 1994, this Philadelphia-based organization has held an annual holiday party for up to 500 inner city children. Santa, local celebrities, music, gifts, arts and crafts, fun, food, and a lot of love have been part and parcel of this all-volunteer event. I have been blessed to have been part of it for several years as my alter-ego faerie clown character, Feather, comes out to play with the kids.

Sacred Paths Community www.sacredpathscommunity.org Sacred Paths Community is an independent, contemporary, non-profit, non-denominational, multi-faith spiritual organization.

SARK www.planetsark.com Susan Ariel Rainbow Kennedy is a fanciful artist, author, and a self-proclaimed "succulent wild woman" who views napping as an art. It is from her that I learned to live juicy!

Sole Purpose Community www.solepurposecommunity.com The dynamic Beverlee Garb is the force behind this site that offers guidance to "awaken to the mystery of your life purpose!" She is a life coach, writer, and speaker.

Scripting for Success www.scriptingforsuccess.com Ruth Anne Wood helps people to "get their dreams out of the drawer," guiding new and seasoned authors to create group/co-authored products such as books, plays, seminars, and movies in ten weeks or less, including her movie that I had the joy of co-directing.

Seva Retreat www.sevaretreat.com Seva retreat is beautiful haven near Philadelphia where events ranging from Barefoot Boogies to concerts, yoga classes, and workshops are held.

Spectrum Health Consulting www.spectrumhealthconsulting.com
Susie Beiler is a board certified holistic health counselor and occupational therapist whose relationship with food takes on a dynamic quality. When she speaks about the importance of nutrition, you can literally taste the freshness!

Rabbi Rami Shapiro www.rabbirami.com Rami is a spiritual teacher, pundit, and writer who espouses a sense of Divine connection beyond traditional bounds. He was my Rabbi for several years while living in Florida.

Rabbi Rayzel Raphael www.shechinah.com/grr/rabbi.html Rayzel is a rainbow of light whose music and ritual inspire and empower. She is a recording artist and performer, workshop facilitator, and community leader.

Shared Heart Foundation www.sharedheart.org Barry and Joyce Vissell are authors of numerous books on life, love, and relationships as well as nurturing and empowering workshop presenters. Their 45-year relationship is an inspiration to many.

Elaine Silver www.elainesilver.com Faerie Elaine Silver is multi-talented singer-songwriter and entertainer for children of all ages.

Soulshaping www.soulshaping.com Jeff Brown is a cleverly creative, wildly word wrangling former lawyer and the author of *Soulshaping: A Journey of Self-Creation*. His weekly inspiration can be viewed on *Good Morning America*.

The Angel Pin Lady www.teamofangels.com Patricia Gallagher might well be an angel herself, with a heart as big as the world as she presents her angel pins to those in need.

The New Seminary www.newseminary.org "Never instead of, always in addition to," is the motto for the interfaith seminary through which I was ordained in 1999.

Transformational Resources www.transformationalresources.com
Peggy Tileston is therapist and educator who assists individuals and

groups in navigating *away* from beliefs and behaviors that cause suffering and *towards* ways of thinking and daily practices that build resiliency and well-being—in all aspects of their lives.

Twilight Wish Foundation www.twilightwish.org Cass Forkin is the powerful and passionate force behind this organization that grants heartfelt wishes to seniors in need. Their motto is, "Help make America a nicer place to age, one wish at a time."

V-Day www.vday.org Founded by author and playwright Eve Ensler, this organization is a global movement to end violence against women and girls.

Veda Conservatory www.vedaconservatory.com "Mukti" Michael Buck is the founder/director and senior teacher of the Vedic Conservatory. He is celebrated as an accomplished instructor's instructor in the art of Thai-Yoga Bodywork.

Dr. Darren Weissman www.drdarrenweissman.com Darren is the creator of The Lifeline Technique, which is a complete body-mind-spirit modality that addresses symptoms as a way of communicating what may be out of balance and needing attention. Darren also incorporates the concept of Infinite Love and Gratitude as a universal healing frequency.

David Wilcox www.davidwilcox.com David is a singer-songwriter whose music has matched the landscape of my life for the past few decades.

Wisdom Magazine www.wisdom-magazine.com is dedicated to opening people's hearts and minds to the philosophies, products, and services of the new millennium. With four regional editions, it is also available online. I have been an interviewer with this publication for many years.

Phyllis Wright www.phylliswrightart.com Phyllis is a graphic artist and art teacher who inspires her students and friends with the love of creativity. Her prints are lush and vivid—and her photography, evocative.

Annabella Wood www.annabellawood.com Annabella is a unique blend of tough and tender, having been a long distance truck driver for 30 years who sings of love and spirituality. Her song "Truck Drivin' Mama" can be seen on YouTube.

WXPN 88.5 FM www.xpn.org This member supported non-commercial radio from The University of Pennsylvania is #1 on the dial in my car, what I wake up to on my alarm clock, and what I play in my office.

Zoetic Workshops www.zoeticworkshops.com Zoetic Workshops Incorporated is dedicated to transforming human consciousness from the Spirit within. Liora Hill is the guide along the way.

Additional Works Referenced

Foreword
Viktor E. Frankl, *Man's Search For Meaning: An Introduction To Logotherapy*, (Beacon Press, 1959).

Intro
"Impostor Syndrome," Wikipedia, 2010, Wikimedia Foundation, Inc. Page was last modified on 7 March 2011 at 21:59. http://en.wikipedia.org/wiki/Impostor_syndrome.
Marianne Williamson, *A Return to Love: Reflections on the Principles of 'A Course in Miracles'*, (Harper Collins, 1992), [From Chapter 7, Section 3].
Paul H. Ray and Sherry Ruth Anderson, *The Cultural Creatives: How 50 Million People Are Changing The World* (Harmony Books, 2000). www.culturalcreatives.org.
Richard Bach, *Illusions: The Adventures of A Reluctant Messiah*, (Dell Publishing, 1977).
Forrest Gump, (Paramount Pictures, 1994).

Chapter 1
"Do-Re-Mi," *The Sound of Music*, Dir. Robert Wise. Robert Wise, 1965.

"Artistic Inspiration" Wikipedia, 2010, Last updated May 1, 2011, Wikimedia Foundation, Inc., http://en.wikipedia.org/wiki/Artistic_inspiration.

Chapter 3
"God is In," Words by Billy Jonas, Laura Mahr, & Chris Chandler. Music by Billy Jonas, 1998, Billy Jonas Bang-A-Bucket Music, BMI.

Chapter 5
"Heigh-Ho," *Snow White and the Seven Dwarfs*, Dir. William Cottrell, David Hand, Wilfred Jackson, Larry Morey, Perce Pearce, Ben Sharpsteen. Walt Disney Productions, 1937. www.nothingbutyoga.com/5th-chakra.html, copyright 2003-2004, NothingButYoga.com.
Interview with Anodea Judith, *Wisdom Magazine*, September 2008.

Chapter 6
"Get up and Go," Words collected, adapted and set to original music by Pete Seeger (1960) TRO (c) 1964 (renewed) Melody Trails Inc., New York, NY.

Chapter 7
Elizabeth Gilbert, *Eat, Pray, Love: One Woman's Search for Everything Across Italy, India and Indonesia*, (Viking, 2006).
Rod Stewart and Ronnie Wood, "Every Picture Tells A Story," Universal Music, 1971.

Chapter 9
"San Francisco (Be Sure to Wear Flowers in Your Hair)," written by John Phillips of The Mamas and The Papas, sung by Scott McKenzie, Ode Records, May 13, 1967.
Sera Beak, *The Red Book: A Deliciously Unorthodox Approach To Igniting Your Divine Spark*, (Jossey-Bass, 2006).

Chapter 10
Billy Steinberg and Tom Kelly, "True Colors," from the Cindy Lauper album *True Colors* (Epic Records, 1986).

Chapter 13
Robin Sharma, *The Monk Who Sold His Ferrari: A Fable About Fulfilling Your Dreams & Reaching Your Destiny*, (Harper Collins Publishers, 1999).

Chapter 14
Jalal Al-Din Rumi, translated by Coleman Barks, "The Guest House," *The Illuminated Rumi*, (Random House Publishing, 1997).
"Higher Love," Steve Winwood and Will Jennings, from *Back In The High Life*, (Island Records, 1986).

Chapter 15
Under The Tuscan Sun, (Touchstone Pictures, September 2003).

Chapter 16
"We Are All Angels," *Songs of the Spirit II*, © Copyright-Tay Toones Record Label. Karen Drucker, 2001.

Chapter 17
Peter Makena, "So Much Magnificence," (Open Sky Music, 1978).

Chapter 18
Elizabeth Lesser, *Broken Open: How Difficult Times Can Help Us Grow*, (Villard Books, Random House, 2005).

Chapter 19
Daily Good, http://www.dailygood.org/more.php?n=3583, 2010.

Chapter 20
Ben Lee, "What's So Bad (About Feeling Good)?," (New West Records, LLC, 2008).

Chapter 22
The Orlons, "South Street," 1963, Dave Appell, Kal Mann, (Cameo Parkway, 1963).
Barry, Robin, and Maurice Gibb. "Stayin' Alive," produced by the Bee Gees, Albhy Galuten, and Karl Richardson (RSO, 1977).

Chapter 25
SQuire Rushnell, *When God Winks On Love*, (Atria Books, 2004).
Julia Cameron, *The Artist's Way*, (Jeremy P. Tarcher/Putnam, 1992).

Chapter 28
Beetlejuice, (The Geffen Company, 1988).

Chapter 29
Albert E. Brumley, "I'll Fly Away," (Hartford Music company in a collection titled *Wonderful Message*, 1932).
Shelby Lynne, "Gotta Get Back," from *I Am Shelby Lynne* (Mercury/Island Records, 1999).
SARK, *Glad No Matter What: Transforming Loss and Change Into Gift And Opportunity*, (New World Library, 2010).

Chapter 31

An Interview with His Holiness the Dalai Lama

Originally published in the October 2008 issue of Wisdom Magazine

The rising temperature on a mid-July early morn couldn't come close to matching the warmth in the hearts of those gathered in the courtyard of the Kalmyk Temple of Saint Zokava at the Kalmyk Brotherhood Society in a working class neighborhood in Philadelphia. The radiance of the sun was eclipsed by that of the sparkle in the eyes of the man for whom several hundred people waited hours to catch a glimpse. An eclectic blend of humanity ranged from infants held in laps to elders sitting in the shade, dressed in rainbow-hued Tibetan and Kalmyk attire and Western garb.

Kalmyks are ethnic Mongolians who are in alignment with Tibetan Buddhism. It was they who issued the invitation for His Holiness to come to Philadelphia for the first time in 18 or so years.

Multi-colored Tibetan prayer flags draped the back of the courtyard and a vine encrusted brick wall bore a yellow and teal colored banner that read in Tibetan "The Philadelphia Tibetan Association Welcomes His Holiness the Dalai Lama, the Reincarnation of Avalokiteshvara ['Embodiment of Compassion' in Tibetan Buddhism]. We Are Very Blessed For Your Visit." This was translated for me by a young IT consultant named Dorjee who had traveled from Texas for the occasion. Visitors arrived from all corners of the globe to celebrate the arrival of this human symbol of grace in the midst of turmoil.

The 73-year-old political and spiritual leader of a government in exile now resides in Dharamsala, India, since the 1959 takeover of his motherland of Tibet by the Chinese government. He seems to view the world as his home.

The aroma of sweet incense wafted through the air, mirrored only by the sounds of lilting music that filled the courtyard, creating the atmosphere for what was to transpire shortly. There was a sense of respectful anticipation, and when His Holiness the 14th Dalai Lama stepped out of the limousine, a sharp intake of breath was audible and a reverent sense of welcome palpable. In a presentation before those gathered, His Holiness spoke of the Kalmyk culture needing to continue through education of the next generation, since many of their elders were moving on to their next incarnation. Listening with rapt attention, mala (prayer beads) ran through the fingers of those in the seats inside the temple as well as those still standing in the courtyard, His Holiness' message being transmitted through speakers so all could hear. At the completion of the morning's event, a red prayer cord and Borstk, which is a traditional Kalmyk pastry, was blessed by His Holiness and offered to the departing crowd.

Later in the day, in the elegant Verizon Hall in the Kimmel Center, a capacity crowd filled the seats as they enjoyed elaborately costumed and choreographed Kalmyk and Tibetan folk music and dances, as well as monotonal Tibetan chanting offered by the Drepung Gomang monks who travel the world to create exquisite sand mandalas, which when complete are disassembled to represent the Buddhist concept of impermanence.

To the sound of thundering applause, His Holiness walked on stage, bowed three times, and then prostrated himself before the image of the Buddha emblazoned on a 50-foot-tall tapestry, known as a thangka. Taking off his sandals, he nestled cross-legged in a radiantly orange chair to begin his teachings on "Buddhism in the 21st Century." His first words indicated that he was "very happy to be here once more in this famous city," and then he made reference to the Liberty Bell and encouraged people to "fill up the crack with our own efforts."

The Dalai Lama indicated that Buddhism reflects three components: "Science, philosophy and religion, but the top priority is unity, to minimize fear and hatred and increase love, compassion and forgiveness."

After the presentation, His Holiness was surprised by a large sheet cake in celebration of his 73rd birthday on July 6th. A delighted smile spread across his face, as he seemed not to be aware of the ritual of blowing out the candle. He then cut a large piece from the middle of the cake and ate with great enthusiasm. There was plenty left to share with his guests in the lobby as they exited the building, enjoying what seemed like manna from heaven. I was happy to receive the last available piece which I 'shared' with my mother over the phone. What a joy it was to have her vicariously experience this milestone with me, albeit 1200 miles away in Florida.

Greg Schultz, of Glenside, PA, who was the manager of the event at the Kimmel Center, describes himself as a practicing Tibetan Buddhist and close friend of the Tibetan people. He offered the following thoughts:

> *His Holiness' message of peace and non-violence as being internal rather than external resonates deep within my very being. There was a moment when he greeted me with a gentle embrace with his head nestled on my shoulder and mine on his. This lasted for what seemed several minutes and left me feeling infinite joy and deep gratitude for all humanity.*

For this journalist, what occurred the next day fulfilled a 20-year-long dream, that of interviewing His Holiness. Ushered into a hotel room past a gauntlet of Philadelphia police officers and secret service agents, I found myself face-to-face with a man whose image had surrounded me for the interceding years, as I had set intention for this day to occur. Immersing myself in the manifestation process with his photo in my car, on a wall in my office, and on several vision boards I created over the years, the seed planting had blossomed into an exquisite garden.

A delightful twinkle appeared in his eyes as he made contact with mine, which at that moment, were filling with tears. I approached him, katah (a traditional white silk scarf) in hand to complete a ritual which involved holding it in prayer pose across my hands. He bowed, took it from me, blessed it, draped it around my neck, and then drew me into a hug. He then motioned for me to sit nearby to begin our conversation. Periodically, His Holiness would reach over to touch my arm to make a point.

Despite speaking fluent English, a translator was nearby to offer assistance when His Holiness searched for the occasional word. His speech is lilting and not always in keeping with grammatic flow. I have maintained the form of communication he used, for authenticity and to offer the flavor of the conversation. My intention is for readers to see the man behind the icon. He shared that he sleeps eight or nine hours per night, completes work at 4:30 p.m. each day, eats no dinner, and then arises at 3:30 a.m. for several hours of meditation. Much of his work now is teaching, less as the political leader and more in the professorial and spiritual roles.

Edie: How do you, as a human being, embody the spiritual—and as a spiritual being, embody the human?

Dalai Lama: I'm nothing special, just an ordinary human being. That's why I always describe myself as a simple Buddhist monk. Different people describe me in a different ways. Some describe me as the living Buddha. Nonsense. Some describe me as 'God-king.' Nonsense. Some consider me as a demon or a wolf in Buddhist robes. That also, I think nonsense. I am simply just one monk. That's all. Then here, the certain temple rule, this seems to me to have a certain responsibility to look after the well-being of society and look after Buddhism and culture. I consider these part of the practice of spirituality. There is no competition between spiritual practice and party politics. That is outdated. We already, since 2001, have elected political position. My position is semi-retired. I am looking forward to complete retirement.

Edie: What would complete retirement look like for you?

Dalai Lama: More time to meditate and preparation for next life. I have three commitments. Number one commitment is promotion of human value. Number two commitment is promotion of race harmony. Number three commitment is about Tibet. My retirement is the third commitment. The previous two commitments, to my death, I have committed.

Edie: What brings you joy?

Dalai Lama: Joy, I think, talking with people and my own motivation is sincere. I consider others as just brothers and sisters. Nothing barrier. I think you notice, like yesterday, when I talk to a few thousand people, I just feel I am talking to an old friend. Like that. I never felt some kind of distance, so therefore, I feel one source of happiness. In that kind of atmosphere, my experience seems some benefit to some people. I feel like my life is something purposeful. Many people have told me that after they listen to my talk, some point which I made, they got certain ideas and their whole life is changed. They are happier. One scientist had discussions about love and compassion. Usually, he felt irritation. After our meeting, for some months, anger never come.

Edie: You speak a great deal about compassion. It seems easy to have compassion for those we feel are like ourselves. When faced with those whose values feel different or even threatening, how can we allow for that same type of understanding?

Dalai Lama: Basically, there are not much differences. They also want happy life. Their method is different. On secondary level, always differences. Faith differences, culture differences, racial differences. Even within one person, yesterday and today, there are differences. We must look at a deeper level. I feel many problems that we are facing, are man-made problems, we have too much emphasis on this secondary thing, forgetting our foundation. At foundation, we are the same human being and we are sharing the same planet. Six billion human beings' future is my future and my future is never separate from the future of six billion human beings. Those people, whose early life, due to lack of affection, always have suspicion and distrust and always remain distant. They never open their heart to other people. I met an American lady many years ago, much distant. Then I told her about my own difficult experiences and I showed some genuine concern. She responded, 'Why are you so concerned about me?' We need more patience. At a fundamental level, we are the same human brothers and sisters. Then forget it. The human mind is very strange. Like that.

Edie: How can we communicate that affection to those who cross our paths and so create a more peaceful planet?

Dalai Lama: Real affection comes from the face. Those political leaders, when they meet, they are always hugging, but not very genuine. Deep, sincerity comes from face and eye. When you entered, you showed that face. I thought, 'This is sincere. Not political hugging.'

Edie: No, definitely not political hugging. As you recently celebrated your 73rd birthday, I wonder what legacy you want to leave.

Dalai Lama: No, no, no. Many years ago, a *New York Times* journalist asked me that question. I told her, as a Buddhist practitioner, not allowed. If I take serious my legacy, that means self-centered. So, I answer that and then again that lady asked a second time and I answered same way and then a third time and then I lost my temper. If you ask, I may lose my temper. (Laughter followed.) Your motivation should be sincere and your life should be of benefit to some people. That is the main thing. Don't care after my death.

Edie: The question wasn't referring to you as an important figure, but about making a difference in people's lives every day, that one among six billion. I won't ask you again. We're friends; I don't want to spoil that.

Although the photographers' camera shutters were clicking away throughout the entire interview, a memorable moment came near the end, when, seemingly posing playfully for the camera, His Holiness leaned back in his chair and, with arms behind his head, allowed a last peal of joyous laughter to echo forth, with such gusto that the ripples could reach the homeland that he envisions awaiting his peoples' return.

To learn more, visit www.dalailama.com.

Afterword

As I type the last few words of this book, I am again filled with mixed emotion, as I was when it was conceived. Excitement, anticipation, and joy, intermingled with *uh-oh, now what?* The difference is that when I began this journey, I had more doubt than certainty; I was dragging my feet, reluctant to take that leap for fear of being in free fall. Now my tootsies are dancing with de-light and I am in free flight. This book 'wrote me', as life lives and breathes me. More present than ever, in the here-and-now precious moment.

Thank you for being companions on the journey and witnessing my unfolding. Perhaps you have found my journey's steps to be much like yours. It is my deepest dream that you carry with you the gems you have gathered along the way, scattering them like colorful treasures for those who accompany you on your personal path. We are now family of choice. I invite you to share with me what you have learned about yourself as a result of reading the book.

In closing, I offer you an abundance of love, all the joy your heart can hold, and then some. May you always recognize the Bliss Mistress or Bliss Master in the mirror.

Bliss Mistress Groups

I invite you to use this book as a jumping-off point for creating your own Bliss Mistress groups in which you can share ideas and foster conversation about what it means to you to live a rich, full, juicy life. The questions that follow each chapter can be used to encourage further inquiry into ways you can move from where you are to where you desire to be.

Transform the Ordinary Into the Extraordinary

Rev. Edie Weinstein, MSW, LSW is a Renaissance woman and Bliss Mistress who delights in inviting people to live rich, full, juicy lives. Edie is an internationally recognized, sought after, colorfully creative journalist, interviewer, and author. A dynamic and inspiring speaker, licensed social worker, and interfaith minister, she offers uniquely designed spiritual rituals. She speaks on the subjects of wellness, spirituality, sexuality, creativity, time management, recovery, body image, mind-fullness, self-esteem, stress management, re-creating yourself, caring for the caregiver, loss, and grief. She is a frequent guest on radio and television, and she enjoys being on the other side of the microphone.

Interviews include the following: His Holiness The Dalai Lama, Louise Hay, Dr. Judith Orloff, Arielle Ford, Wayne Dyer, Deepak Chopra, Marianne Williamson, Joan Borysenko, Grover Washington, Jr., Patch Adams, Rev. Michael Beckwith, Neale Donald Walsch, Jean Houston, Michael Franti, Elizabeth Lesser, Barnet Bain, Debbie Ford, Glen Velez, Lori Cotler, Will Arntz, E. Raymond Brown, Ben & Jerry, and SARK.

"Edie is a wonderful, insightful, fun interviewer who made me instantly feel at home. She puts her heart, mind and soul into the interview which makes it heartfelt and powerful. Her skill is unmistakable and her spirit is beautiful."—Judith Orloff MD, author of Second Sight

"Edie is a source of brilliant loving energy that meets people's needs and serves for everyone's mutual support and growth. She is a Cuddle Party facilitator of the highest caliber serving a wide area of the Mid-Atlantic Region. I would trust her to give 100% to any common goal or project she would say "YES" to along the way."—Len Daley, Executive Director, EDUCO, Inc. Foundations of Facilitation

"Edie is one remarkable woman. Her spirit can lift boulders, her warmth can heat mid-sized cities, her personality has more snap, crackle and pop than . . . well, you know what. Edie interviewed me for Wisdom Magazine. She's a brilliant writer and a deft interviewer. I heartily recommend her for whatever project or opportunity you have in mind."—Paul Stone, Director of Advertising, W.B. Mason Company

"Edie is one those rare unforgettable women who is so delightful that you find yourself looking for projects to collaborate with her on. Her writing talent is undeniable, having interviewed luminaries such as HH The Dalai Lama. But what's more, Edie brings her full-out shining essence to everything she creates in her business. You will want her on your team!"—Gina Mazza, Owner, Epiphany Works, LLC

Edie is a contributor to Beliefnet, with her daily Bliss Blog
http://features.beliefnet.com/blissblog
Contact her today to see how she can meet the needs of your organization or publication.
www.liveinjoy.org   www.cuddleparty.com
You can find her on Facebook, LinkedIn, and Twitter

Bliss Bravos

"Edie Weinstein is one of those rare people who've learned to live her bliss and now, fortunately, she's shared her secrets in *The Bliss Mistress Guide to Transforming the Ordinary into the Extraordinary*. Readers will be delighted and nurtured by her 'bliss bites' as they learn how to discover their own special bliss through Weinstein's open sharing of her tools and techniques, designed to bring out the bliss in everyone. She's the real deal. Grab this book." —Jim Donovan, author of *52 Ways to a Happier Life*

"Even those of us who believe that life is a journey and that uncomfortable or painful experiences are only opportunities for growth, can have the tendency to see our spiritual growth as somehow apart from day-to-day life and its ordinary annoyances. Edie, a genuine Bliss Mistress if there ever was one, has a way of being in life that naturally elevates those annoying moments into the realm of the sacred . . . while gracefully keeping The Sacred free of any pretension. She brings new meaning to the power of 'just being yourself' . . . and I bless her for being a role model for all of us when 'just being yourself' shouldn't be so challenging, but humanly, just plain is." —Nancy Dreyfus, Psy.D., author of *Talk to Me Like I'm Someone You Love*

"Honest and insightful, Bliss Mistress Edie Weinstein's well-crafted book, *The Bliss Mistress Guide to Transforming the Ordinary into the Extraordinary* shows readers how they can break through limiting false beliefs and re-frame even their darkest Kodak Moments into portraits of vivid color, bursting with joy and love . . . total Bliss! Broken down into thirty easily digestible 'Bliss Bites', readers can choose to savor Edie's rich nuggets of wisdom, **distilled** from her own personal experience, on a daily basis, or indulge all at once in a marathon transformational pig-out." —Mary Arsenault, publisher of *Wisdom Magazine*

"*The Bliss Mistress Guide* is a treasure trove of 'pleasure bites' to inspire your own playful upward path into a life of greater meaning and joy. The Bliss Mistress herself is masterful at transforming adversity into opportunity, and she can help you do the same. If you feel impelled to squeeze the juice out of every life experience, you must read this book." —Gina Mazza, journalist, editor, creative muse, and author of *Everything Matters, Nothing Matters: For Women Who Dare to Live with Exquisite Calm, Euphoric Creativity & Divine Clarity*

"Eavesdrop on the 'Bliss Mistress', this internationally sought after speaker, writer, facilitator and journalist who understands, 'Well behaved women rarely make history'! Laugh and muse in delight as Edie turns her adversities into blissful adventures. I love how Edie teaches us how to hand your monkey mind a banana to quiet the inner critic and move beyond limiting beliefs that keep us from our bliss. Enjoy her personal self discoveries, powerful questions and tools to access your bliss as you discover more ways to celebrate being a god or goddess having a blissful experience!" —Ruth Anne Wood, playwright, success trainer, and host of the transformational www.LiveYourPeace.com interview series

"There is divine alchemy afoot! Mix one part self made renaissance woman, one part lovely clown, one part open hearted social worker, one part inspiring writer and one part juicy goddess and you have Edie Weinstein. She will tickle your spirit, move you to happy tears and share the secrets to creating the bliss filled life you deserve!" —Rev. Victor Fuhrman

"Nobody but Edie Weinstein could have written this book. She has overcome challenges that would have floored anyone else yet truly radiates happiness and healing to anyone lucky enough to meet her—and now she shares her secrets in this book. Written with the warmth and understanding of human frailty that characterizes real compassion, this book will help you plug into the energy that sustains and supports a fulfilling life rich with possibility." —Jenny Wade, Ph.D., author of *Transcendent Sex: When Lovemaking Opens the Veil* and *Changes of Mind: A Holonomic Theory of the Evolution of Consciousness.*

"If ever there were a person born to beat the flannel-covered drum of Cuddle Party and to make the world a more snuggl-o-icious, blissful place, it's Edie Weinstein! Her abilities to share courageously, and role model that bliss and happiness are our birthright, are inspiring. And now, with *The Bliss Mistress Guide to Transforming the Ordinary into the Extraordinary*, Edie's made her contagious enthusiasm available in surrogate form, ready for your eyes and spirit to devour, just in case you're out of range for one of her extraordinary hugs!" —Reid Mihalko of ReidAboutSex.com, sex and relationship expert, and co-creator of Cuddle Party

"It's about time this brilliance was written down and shared with the world! Edie Weinstein and her alter ego, The Bliss Mistress, have created a fantastic little book about courage and love, and how to make the most of each moment of each day. The Bliss Mistress' fearless take on life has inspired me, over and over again, to push my own edges, to try new things, to find the little nugget that turns a wacky adventure into a source of nurturing for my soul. This book (and Edie's life) is a reminder that having a joyous, blissful, wondrous life is not about avoid challenges, but rather engaging with life fully and enthusiastically, and finding the Yes in all of it!" —Marcia Baczynski, president and founder of www.AskingForWhatYouWant.com, and co-creator of Cuddle Party

"Having read Edie's essays, interviews and articles for many years, I am one of her fans who has always asked 'when are you going to write a book?' Edie has so much to share, in such a succulent heart-felt way, that her musings beckon for a wider audience. I am thrilled that the Bliss Mistress has been born." —Susan Duval, founder of Susan Duval Seminars for Personal Growth, Holistic Health, Healing, Spirituality and Metaphysics

"I was delighted to hear that Edie Weinstein had written a book. She has long been at the center of things, connecting people in the most helpful ways and being a force that leads us all to our bliss. At the beginning she asks asks the reader to take an inventory on our current state of bliss. Thus begins a wonderful journey that focuses not on money, power and societal pressure, but on that most beautiful of frequencies, bliss. With a playfully provocative nature, Edie challenges us to create a 'loving you list'. This is one of many delicious exercises that invite us to take control of our lives and to move 'living with bliss' to the top of our priorities. Edie is a kindred spirit to Rumi, who once said, 'Either give me enough wine or leave me alone'! Take Edie's challenge and find your bliss." —Michael London, singer-songwriter and recording artist of *The Field* and *The Soul Wakes*

"There is always the thought that with so many new-agey-self-help books out there that there are no new ideas. Well just wait until you read Edie Weinstein's book; *The Bliss Mistress Guide to Transforming the Ordinary into the Extraordinary*. That is exactly what she did; transform ideas that we have about life, and what is bliss into wonderful, magical gems and examples that will transform anyone! I am sure that people will be blessed by her humor, wisdom, and how she is an inspiration to live a blissful life." —Karen Drucker, recording artist and author of *Let Go of the Shore—Stories and Songs that Set The Spirit Free*

"What a delightful, upbeat, inspiring gift Edie Weinstein offers! *The Bliss Mistress Guide* is filled with heart-centered wisdom and lots of down-to-earth, believable, practical examples from the life of a woman who has chosen to find joy and multiply it by sharing. I expect that you will be lifted and moved to live your own bliss by dancing through these pages. Thank you Edie." —Alan Cohen, author of *A Daily Dose of Sanity*

"Edie Weinstein wrote this book to be a conversation. Like all good conversations it engages and transforms. I was drawn into her tales, touched by her insights, and called to see my own life through the bliss lens of her life. A wonderful book to read; a marvelous conversation to have." —Rabbi Rami, author of *Recovery—The Sacred Art*

"Nora Roberts wrote 'overcoming is not the same as getting over'. That phrase could have been created for Edie Weinstein. She is like a bouncing ball, coming back from whatever challenges life has presented to her—they are many and diverse. Bliss Mistress describes her perfectly. She creates loving auras and her level of passion is of the Highest Good! Having known Edie for eons it seems and having witnessed her methods of dealing with life's changes, I have often been in awe of her capacity to turn a negative into a positive. This book is part of her personal dream—to be able to share life's joys with people who are unaware of them. She has a simplistic approach which is breathtakingly refreshing from some of the complicated, mind twisting writings regarding taking care of oneself. Best of all is her humour. We enjoyed many hysterical laughs together, once when I was in the car with her and was complaining of back ache. She went to work on my shoulders using imagery and visualisation. My eyes were closed and there she was rubbing my neck. Apparently people were walking by and peering into the odd scene. We could hardly breathe for laughter—and the stress just went away. That's Edie. Multifaceted, mysterious at times, loyal friend, beautiful soul. In one word—FUN. What more would one want from a book? It makes life so much more exciting, sweet, loving and yes, educational. Bliss—with Edie: I see her as Beautiful Luscious Interactive Superb and if I may return to my British origin—Smashing! That's Bliss. Thank you for making the world a more charming place. Such a cuddler too. We do not need central heating when Edie is around. Thank you for opening my mind to a different attitude toward BLISS! —Yvonne Kaye Ph.D., author, speaker, and interfaith minister

"Edie Weinstein cuddles the reader as she writes her juicy stories. There is a direct personal and authentic contact that permeates her writing. The stories are exquisite and full of taste and texture. A book not only worth reading but savoring as well." —Dr. Murray Needleman, clinical psychologist and radio talk show host

"Edie has created a lovely and beautifully crafted treasure trove of deliciously satisfying 'Bliss Bites'. This journey she takes us all on is better than 'S'mores In Heaven' and a 'Cosmic Yes' combined. This precious sojourn has her fabulous imprint and powerful DNA embedded through this appropriately titled guide. This is such an important map (divinely created by the Bliss Mistress) for all of our 'Inner GPS' to integrate and trust at our Core level so we can ultimately experience that state of bliss that we all deserve." —Brian Hilliard, Conscious Heart-trepreneur and Lover of Life (and all things Arielle Ford)

"Joseph Campbell urged us to 'follow our bliss'. Edie's new book shows us how 'bliss' is our natural state of being." —Barry Vissell, MD and Joyce Vissell, RN, MS, authors of *The Shared Heart, Models of Love*, and *A Mother's Final Gift*

"I feel in-couraged and invited in by this wonderful book. Edie has an uncanny ability to make you feel right at home when you read her. We are all sitting around the hearth, munching on sweets, sharing our stories, reminding each other that we can find our bliss everywhere, in the quiet space between the breaths, and in the connection between our hearts. Here we are, sharing our humanness, remembering . . . What a lovely read." —Jeff Brown, weekly contributor to *Good Morning America*, and author of *Soulshaping: A Journey of Self-Creation* and *Apologies to the Divine Feminine (from a warrior in transition)*